No Gods but One

NO GODS BUT ONE

Daniel Berrigan

WILLIAM B. EERDMANS PUBLISHING COMPANY
GRAND RAPIDS, MICHIGAN / CAMBRIDGE, U.K.

Published 2009 by
Wm. B. Eerdmans Publishing Co.
2140 Oak Industrial Drive N.E., Grand Rapids, Michigan 49505 /
P.O. Box 163, Cambridge CB3 9PU U.K.

Printed in the United States of America

15 14 13 12 11 10 09   7 6 5 4 3 2 1

Library of Congress Cataloging-in-Publication Data

Berrigan, Daniel.
No gods but One / Daniel Berrigan.
p.   cm.
ISBN 978-0-8028-6462-8 (pbk.: alk. paper)
1. Bible. O.T. Deuteronomy — Commentaries.   I. Title.

BS1275.53.B47   2009
222'.15077 — dc22

2009026540

www.eerdmans.com

To Philip, Elmer, Mary, Tom, John, Peter, Larry.
Rest in peace. You taught, and more.

A Note on the Use of Scripture in This Volume

The basic structure of this text follows the chapter-and-verse structure of Deuteronomy in the NRSV. In the text, Berrigan occasionally uses quotations (sometimes slightly altered) from the NRSV. More often he uses quotations (sometimes slightly altered) from the NAB. And sometimes he is rendering the biblical text in his own poetic equivalent, or creating a rich interplay of different biblical versions.

Chapter-and-verse citations have been used infrequently in the text to keep it as free from technical apparatus as possible.

Those quotations from the New Revised Standard Version of the Bible are copyright © 1989 by the Division of Christian Education of the National Council of Churches of Christ in the U.S.A., and used by permission.

Those quotations from the New American Bible with Revised New Testament and Revised Psalms are copyright © 1991, 1986, 1970 by the Confraternity of Christian Doctrine, Washington, D.C. and are used by permission of the copyright owner. All rights reserved.

Contents

CONTENTS

Introduction: Is the Lost Past the Future Found?

For the sake of the tribe,
Moses set in stone
the tradition of law,
and of the immemorial "choice"
that encircled the people for
centuries, an aura undimmed,
a shekinah of providence,
invincible.

We come to the humane and influential "book of the laws" — better, "book of the second law." A lost book, we learn. And more — and wonderfully — found.

In view of the fate of the book, as it touched on the behavior of believers, one is tempted to amend the "lost and found." Perhaps the matter is put more justly by saying, Our book was totally lost, and only partially found. Once found, however, the scroll was a (seeming) godsend for solicitous King Josiah, vowed as he was to reform his people's behavior.

As to the means of bringing this about, the good king was at sea. What would prod the reform along? The book, the book, that mysterious book! It lay for generations gathering dust in some crevice or corner of the temple.

So the story went. But could there have existed only a single copy? We marvel; our version speaks of only one, the unique, the original.

~

Only one version of the book? But of what use this hidden tome? One might think, by way of analogy, of venerating a dish of manna in the Ark, while a starving people outside the temple lament and beg for food.

One or many copies — still, the implication is plain. Crucial instructions imbedded in the scroll were neglected by the chosen. Self-willed, they strayed far from the ordinances of Moses and the prophets.

~

Then, a momentous discovery: the book lay to hand, revered and scrutinized. By some.

Alas, the "reform" turned out a debacle. Too little and too late, it seemed. Much attention paid to restoration of liturgical and moral niceties, little attention to matters of justice — the fate of the "widow and orphan and stranger at the gate." And no halt to public evils: interminable wars, forced labor. Those idols of greed and violence — they were (and are!) longer-lived than Methuselah.

~

Still, the likes of Jeremiah spoke loud and clear for the true tradition. His oracles (especially chapter 11) show the influence of the "little book that could" — but alas, did not.

~

How name the literary form of the precious scroll? Will this do: "An Old Man's Memories"? Only, one thinks, if an amending phrase is kept in mind, something like "those memories, as here presented."

Deuteronomy has been attributed to Moses; alas, the difficulties against his authorship are all but insurmountable. Apart from legend, no sound evidence exists to support the claim. (And this, though for centuries Moses was presented in the Catholic tradition as author of the entire Pentateuch. The claim is long since buried, along with the bones of its advocates.)

However, denying the authorship to Moses does not dispose of the theory of a single-handed achievement. Donald Akenson is persuasively inventive on the point:

> The editor-cum-author here knew exactly what he was doing. The Book of Deuteronomy is a strong spine with two mighty arms. That spine and those arms can support, on the one hand, the first four Books of Moses, and on the other, the four "Former Prophets" (Joshua, Judges, Samuel, and Kings).
>
> There is a symmetry here that is immensely skillful. The four books on each hand balance each other; and each set of four becomes a set of five because they are thematically and historically integrated with the central volume, Deuteronomy. By using the Book of Deuteronomy in this dual role, the editor-author was carving in his own way two sets of five tablets.
>
> He, the most self-aware of historians, knew full well that he was invoking here the image of the two sets of five laws brought down by Moses from the mountain in the establishment of the Sinai covenant. The use of this image speaks well of the good sense of the inventor; he did not risk Yahweh's wrath for vain-glory by carving out ten scrolls, and thus making himself equal with Moses.
>
> But his nine, presented in the manner he did, was very close, and close enough to tell us that he knew that he, like the Moses whom he depicts in his historical text, was creating a religion that was virtually new.
>
> *Surpassing Wonder: The Invention*
> *of the Bible and the Talmuds*

∼

The task is clear, and awesome. The author-editor must intervene with his own vision, must amend the original oral traditions and documents, arranging and rearranging, completing, adding to and subtracting from. In this skilled shuffling and scissoring, special interests — whether priestly (heavily influential, self-sacrilized), prophetic, royal, or others — undoubtedly collided. And compromised.

And what of that scribe? one wonders. Was he free to set down events suggestive of the falling short of priest, king, or people, of faithlessness? Or did a royal hand descend on his shoulder, bidding him omit episodes of weakness or crime?

Must the tale celebrate a main theme: royal greatness, "honors, riches, and the credit of a great name"?

~

As to the Moses of our text, his story was set down centuries after the events recounted, as has been said before. In the long meantime, memories of Moses grew and proliferated, his image towered aloft, became an icon of legend and folklore, larger than life. First he was revered as a national patron, then a universal patron. In the final apotheosis, he descended the mountain, "horned" with glory.

So the scribal task was formidable. Amid the splendors of conquest and the grandiosities of empire, how tell of beginnings both chancy and blood-ridden? How tell of the towering spirit who set all in motion, forging, out of a ragtag gallimaufry of refugees, an inkling, a first wink of the eye of a prodigious world power — We shall go for it!

~

The book is a pentimento of memory. Only in this sense can we claim Deuteronomy as the "Memories of Moses." Through the founder, whose voice resounds in the text, national glory is vastly enhanced. That glory demands a hero and a visionary who enjoyed direct access to God.

And more, and more; for the sake of the tribe, the same visionary and legislator set in stone the tradition of law, and of the immemorial "choice" that encircled the people for centuries, an aura undimmed, a shekinah of providence, invincible.

A light was struck. No earthly delict, whether infidelity or the brutalities of enslavement and exile, could quench that flame.

~

Through a noble, even superhuman ancestor (in team with his mighty brother), the Exodus of the tribe, together with the accompanying marvels, are rendered unique, alluring. Generations to come will bask in the glory of Moses and Aaron.

So the great story is underway, with the heft, upward and onward, of oral traditions. Perhaps, given the vagaries of time, a question (whether the hero had once existed in the flesh) became irrelevant. Time bore a burnishing and creative hand: an ancestor grew large and larger in the mind, became a "necessary creation."

Another image. If no mortal mother bore the hero, time's urgent womb would serve. The splendor of the imperial achievement at home and abroad, the temple and palace, the accession of kings of the stature of Saul, David, Solomon — these demand a super-ancestor.

~

The chosen arrive in the Land of Promise; they conquer the Canaanites. Confidence and self-approval emerge; given time, a kingship shines bright.

And the theme of glory has darker hues, too, contradictions that place it in question — even deny it. The conflict of spiritual forces is never entirely quenched.

The era of prophets arrives. It introduces far different royalties — towering eminences, severe of mind and speech, unexampled figures of holiness, of frowning brows and fulminations. Kings, beware! Isaiah, Jeremiah, Ezekiel — they point minatory fingers. You, self-declared immune ones, you stand under judgment.

The prophets define sin and sinner anew: "You, king, are the one." Sin, darkly flourishing on high, must be confronted: injustice, tribalism, slaughter in war, meaningless worship. Announce, denounce, no matter the risk!

~

Thus a dominant theme of our book emerges — a war of myths. Prophet versus king.

We note the vaulting ideology of imperialism. Self-justified, glorying in riches, armed might, high culture. ("Solomon in all his glory" — how true the phrase from the lips of Christ. And a put-down implied: that "glory" is less glorious than a common flower of the fields.)

In apogee, it seemed the royal sun would never set. Probed by the fabled Queen of Sheba, Solomon's wisdom exceeds all, touches on every stratum of creation, is minute, abstract, universal, cosmic even. Hyperbolic, stupendous, the myth bursts the boundaries of the human.

Come now! Do we protest?

~

Who will deflate the glory, critique the defaulting line of kings, cry "shame" — the crime, the injustice, the violence that stain the royal escutcheon? The prophets will not be bought or beguiled. For the first time in the Bible, royal behavior falls under judgment human and divine — these mystics being authorized, as they insist, by God.

Inevitably, reprisal follows: fierce royal nay-saying, conflict, the burning of oracles, pursuit, scorn, ostracism, even death.

~

An analogy might be of help. Let us suppose that the scribe yields before a visual artist. Now, rather than being written down, the story will be painted.

The artist may depict the moral scene as a shadowless high noon, a scene by de Chirico, perhaps. The landscape is static, motionless under the sun. Human figures are vertical sticks, trapped in a timeless vertigo, parched, emotionless, stuck.

Then, a second painting: this one bespeaks a passion stilled, plenary, waiting, ready. A figure emerges, solitary, an old king by Rouault, perhaps. This personage has spoken and ruled well and rendered just judgment. Now age overtakes him; the work is done.

His concentration is intense; his look rests within. He holds a plucked flower in hand, all that is left to him. A flower, heal-all, the bloom of truth unfazed; the truth that, despite death and loss, will accompany him into the company of the kings. Better, into the Vision beatific.

PART ONE

REMINISCENCE AND COUNSEL

Moses' First Discourse

The Recollection

Forty Seasons of Discontent (Chs. 1:6–3:29)

Chapter 1

It was

*the fortieth
year,*

*the first day
of*

*the eleventh
month. . . .*

The words, the numbers, are like a held breath. How carefully noted, and how poignant! We near the end of a seemingly endless sojourn, recounted in detail in Exodus and Numbers — and now in Deuteronomy.

We have come so far; we stand so near. Moses stands so near — and yet farthest of all. This side of death, he is forbidden entrance to the Land of Promise, that dearest — and nearest — of rewards. He stands under a fierce indictment, a delict held in secret by the god.

An astonishing irony — a miscarriage of justice? His offense is unknown (unknown to himself?). The consequence is known to all — to all the ages.

No accounting for this God!

~

Moses is circumspect. The god keeps a secret; so will he. In an ever-so-slight reference to his "crime" and its punishment, he says only this to the people (in v. 37):

The Lord
was angered

also
against me,

on
your account,

and
said,

"*Not*
even you

shall
enter
here."

"On your account"? The mystery remains; the delict stands. A harsh sentence is decreed. The classic insider, the man of unparalleled access to the Holy — he will undergo the death of an outsider. Worse — of a reject.

A biblical conundrum, this delict of Moses. One ponders the implication as the pen of our scribe lifts from the page, circumspect. He shakes his head, slowly. No, it shall not be told. Let the dire effect be underscored, the cause left blank.

Is the implication an instance of the deity's double mind regarding his favorite? Has Moses drawn too near, does he know too much, is he too powerful? Does he threaten, all unwitting (or perhaps witting), to play the supplanter? Must he, in consequence, be rudely reminded of his creaturely status?

"Fear God, and grow wise." Indeed, Moses had obeyed the command to the hilt. But, but — did God fear him?

Of all the mysteries that shroud the mystic and lawgiver, this seems the deepest: the deity's ambivalence toward one pre-eminently chosen from among the chosen.

~

At the start of the Moses saga, we were told of an inexplicable, near murderous attack against the favored one. Now, as he nears the end, the grand entrance, triumph is denied him.

~

In the desert years, we recall, Moses and Aaron hardly stood alone in divine disfavor. For a variety of sins, the entire nomadic generation was condemned. The corpse of Moses, together with that of his brother and sister, would be mingled with a vast trail of bones in the wilderness.

Experts have sifted those bones over the centuries, seeking clues as to the traditions surrounding great Moses. The bones keep their secret.

Like the bones of Ezekiel's vision?

No, these bones are different; they refuse to knit together.

~

One example of the inflation of the "legend of beginnings." The priestly scribe of 500 C.E. calculated that Moses led an armed force of some 600,000 men. The number suggests a population of Exodus folk of some 3 million. In *The Old Testament without Illusion*, John McKenzie remarks acidly, "One may calculate that a Hebrew host of this size would have caused an exodus of Egyptians rather than Hebrews."

~

Scholars have likewise sought light on the notorious Mosaic default "at Meriba, by the waters." As noted before, little of substance has come to light. The text, livid with divine anger, is opaque to probing eyes. The god does not easily give away the god's secrets.

~

In the era of Moses, the God of compassion, the God of the prophets, is emerging slowly, painfully, ambiguously, in national consciousness. At least on occasion, the god stands with the oppressed. With due reservations about fiery moods and reprisals, one is grateful for isolated acts of mercy and mitigation.

Still, an ethic of "to-fro" holds firm. Powerful opposing influences are at work. As we approach the imperial era, another god than a champion of the underdog appears. The emerging royal deity is a phobogenic projection, a fabled warrior seizing the reins of history, riding fast and furious.

War after war erupts. And in the era of kings, we note a series of ominous social developments, including, for the first time, an army of conscripts. Forced laborers construct grandiose emblems of empire. Taxation throttles; a class system coddles the wealthy and ignores the poor. Israel, in sum, has become a new and onerous Egypt.

And, crowning all, a pharaonic god. The God of the oppressed is nearly in eclipse, in favor of a god of the oppressor.

~

All, however, is not lost. Indeed, the worst times beget the breakthrough. Kings, whether David, Solomon, Hezekiah, or the royal nonentities who follow — the oppression that is their stock-in-trade brings in its wake an inspired opposition.

We will never have done with hailing them, the grand prophets. They salvage an onerous, odious scene, announcing a radically different God than the official deity of the greedy and violent. More — these passionate truth-tellers hold their rulers accountable for the sin that brought ruin to Egypt: idolatry.

Thus, out of the darkness of a wicked time, a dawn at last: the blessing bestowed on their time (and ours as well) of Isaiah, Jeremiah, and company.

1:6ff.

Our text is a summons to remembrance. In memory lies healing from the world's incursive ills. In memory apprehended and courageously acted on, truth and strength flourish.

~

Firmness and suppleness here, and a deep human sense. It is as though the shade of great Isaiah stood near the scribe, attentive to the voice of Moses.

The address is direct, the memory urgent, the instruction lucid. We had not heard before a command imbedded in a code of law. Probity and compassion, we are told, are hallmarks of a people of faith. "Justice" issuing from "you judges" must be prophetic, unambiguous.

Justice above all! Before the just judge, a stranger at the gate stands equal to a tribesman. Ordinary person or grand personage — no matter; distinctions of class and station are disallowed:

> *Fear*
> *no man,*
>
> *for*
>
> *judgment*
> *is*
> *God's.*

This is the sublime eminence of the judge. With fear and trembling he is appointed, to mime the Event of the last day, the final judgment.

Fear and trembling befit those appointed. And in the community at large, no fear and trembling. Fear only God, who is also named Judge; and who one day will judge the judges.

One can hardly conjure a more awesome vocation.

~

And in our day and place, one could scarcely summon a status more corrupted in practice, more entailed and betrayed, more sunk in racism and cronyism, in special interests and suppression of truth.

American judges? From the Supreme Court down, many of the incumbents are in servitude to a culture of death.

How, in a deadly atmosphere, are works of justice to flourish with independence of mind and needful passion? The contrast between the biblical injunction and American judicial behavior could hardly be more stark.

~

And we wonder: What inspires this voice of Moses, sounding forth with such clarity? The text, we are told, was set down in a woeful time. The institution of judges had long since proven decadent — and the kingship as well. It is as though, against all odds, a century of mayhem had sought to retrieve a golden age — alas, long gone.

Somehow, someone intervened, perhaps to underscore a truth lost in wicked times. Something like this: Granted, juridical misbehavior is the ugly norm. No matter; rendering justice with compassion must be insisted on. Long neglected, abandoned in practice, justice as a peerless civic virtue must be taught and underscored anew.

Let the text be set down, a reproach and a judgment. Do the words invoke a ghost rather than a robust reality? So be it. But let the ghost, summoned as it were to the bar, grow solid flesh and bone. Let the resurrected bear witness against shame and high crime, let him summon a humane and heartfelt sense of the neighbor.

~

In a given culture, judges illustrate the flourishing or decline of ideal and practice. In the times of the text, the magistrates have fallen away from justice, have bartered away their birthright. Inevitably, they oppose as well the justice of God. They must be made accountable once more, must repent and undergo conversion.

Let the text lie open, a summons.

~

Another text, of a later, hardly lesser poet. He takes the guise of a species of (black-robed?) cynic, urging a like sour spirit on others:

Child of Europe, Part IV
Grow your tree of falsehood from a single grain of truth.
Do not follow those who lie in contempt of reality.

Let your lie be even more logical than the truth itself,
So the weary travelers may find repose in the lie.

After the Day of the Lie, gather in select circles,
Shaking with laughter when our real deeds are mentioned.

Dispensing flattery called: perspicacious thinking.
Dispensing flattery called: a great talent.

We, the last who can still draw joy from cynicism.
We, whose cunning is not unlike despair.

A new, humorless generation is now arising.
It takes in deadly earnest all we received with laughter.

Czeslaw Milosz

~

One lingers with intense longing over the instruction of Moses.

O for a better way, a more humane behavior! Emotions stir the heart, movements akin to those evoked by the text. A like summoning of integrity and compassion was once claimed as our moral armature. We have squandered a grand legacy. We must assemble as one, and mourn it.

We would have our children and their children know: Forbidden virtues are honored in our hearts — if not in our behavior.

1:34-40

The old man's memories meander hither and yon, in free association. There is no discernible time sequence. Back and back time takes him; he stands once more in the wilderness years. Conflicts with Yahweh stand out like jagged rock formations struck by lightning. And now and then, a very Himalaya rears up; no surmounting it, death on the peak, death on the flanks!

Two of his companions will enter the Land of Promise, but Moses will not. It grieves him unutterably, this dire edict. Why are Caleb and Joshua favored? Joshua will succeed him; must Joshua supplant as well?

Great Moses, alas, must resign himself to falling short, deprived and punished.

And what of the children, born in the wilderness? They will enter the Land of Promise, those who, in a curious phrase,

do not
as yet
know

good
and
evil.

Meaning what? In the eyes of the deity, is this to be accounted a virtue, this "not knowing good and evil"? Perhaps an ironic hearkening back to the scene in Eden, and the temptation of the serpent? There, Eve foolishly entered into conversation with the intruder, skilled in bending the truth to his own devices.

Only listen, he avers, this utterly sincere serpent: The woman and man shall not die for tasting of the fruit of

the tree
of
the knowledge

of
good

and
evil . . .

The curious phrase lingers on unlikely lips — of God and of ha-satan. To the latter, the fruit of the tree oozes sweet promise. It implies no fealty to God — and, for that matter, no death threat.

The Promise is heady as a fruit of paradise: You shall no longer be mere creatures of God. Come up, come higher!

You
shall be

like
God,

knowing
good

and
evil.

∿

In our text, this would seem the implication: The second generation of Exodus have had no part in the divagations of their elders. Knowing the good, the younger have spurned evil.

They have thus merited the Land of Promise. A moment will come, a signal, a blast of the shofar. Cross the river and enter — the grand occasion so long desired, so long delayed!

By supposition — or by hope — or perhaps by foreknowledge — those poised at the river will be honored by the embrace of the deity. They have surpassed the generation of murmuring revolt and idolatry. For them, a Destiny unutterably sweet beckons. Come in, welcome!

1:41-46

Moses, for his part, seems confused regarding the will of the god.

One occasion looms big and dangerous: a resolve to do battle against the Amorites. Obedient or disobedient (we are not told), the chosen gird for battle.

The battle goes badly. And Yahweh, for his part, seems perversely content, like a parent who has let a recalcitrant child fall on its face, somewhat like, "I told you so! Next time, listen to me!"

∿

The geography of the forty-year trek is also confusing, when it is recorded at all. Did the wanderers pass through Sinai from Egypt to arrive in Canaan? The mountains of the Sinai are all but impassable; the surrounding land is a waste. And prior to the fourth century A.D., no identification was made of the route of passage.

We have, in other words, a mythological leader and his tribe, moving like a mirage in an improbable landscape. Surreal, the caravan staggers about under a punishing sun.

And above and beyond, transcendent and awful, reigns the god, whose thunderous blows all but extinguish noon.

17

The people grow heartsick, disoriented. And no wonder. Who can forget (who is allowed to forget) the original sin, and its judgment, weighing heavy from the first days of "freedom"?

You
are
never

to see

freedom
land!

∿

Meantime, how to describe the remaining years of a people proscribed? Life is reduced to a "meantime," a "marking time," a "doing hard time." These are a species of interim people. They come from somewhere, but they will go nowhere. This is the judgment. It is irrevocable; this generation exists only to produce a progeny better than themselves.

Does it bear meaning or no meaning, this scene, the interminable trek (and bearing, perforce, its stigma, a curse)? Trudging and bivouacing, colliding and bickering, faithful, idolatrous — the murmuring, the tent, and the momentous gift of the law. A parable — dire, fabulous, alluring — of the human pilgrimage through time?

∿

That law has come down, a hammer blow. A momentous matter: the law is found wanting, wanting in love. It lacks heart. No wonder, then, if periodic revolt erupts. This restive tribe, their future proscribed, cry out, break out. They have had a surfeit of law, of lawgiver — of Moses.

Chapter 2

2:1-12

A strange mix of truth and falsehood, of aspiration and illusion, of dread, decline, and death, is this cultural matrix, the fabled story of beginnings.

These Israelites, it appears, are not the sole favored descendants of Abraham. The author(s) must take into account large competing interests. And with what surpassing care Yahweh must play his hand, lest a wrong bidding set favorites at the throat of — favorites!

The Edomites, for example, descend from Esau. Hands off them; pass them by. "I will not give you so much as a foot of their land."

Likewise, the Moabites will be spared, for a time. They spring from the tribe of Lot, nephew of Abraham, so they are exempt from the incursion of the would-be settlers: "Do not provoke them. . . . I will give you nothing of their land."

And the response we read: "So we gave a wide berth to the land of our brothers. . . ."

As for the other tribes, outsiders all, they are simply written off. Pereant, full speed ahead.

2:13-37

We have come to the thirty-eighth year of wanderings. The tone is of a dying fall; every one of Moses' generation, "even to the last man," has perished. And what of himself, solitary and aging?

Events that follow are presented austerely, as matters of divine will. "Take it or leave" is the tone. The time of exemptions is ending; lines are drawn firmly. Do armies impede the progress of the chosen? Sweep over, crush them, with utmost violence.

We mourn and are confounded, pondering a history which names itself "sacred."

∼

The "generation of entrance" into the Land of Promise is presented artfully. Behold, a people fully equipped and self-conscious, in possession of law, liturgy, leader, of incontestable armed might, in covenant with a god who guarantees safe passage. On, then, to possession of the land!

~

And today, some thirty centuries after the events, some twenty-five centuries after their recounting, Israelis cling to the original gift of the land.

Palestinians — who might they be? They are no more favored than the early Amorites:

> I
> *now deliver*
> *into your hands*
> *Sihon*
>
> *the Amorite*
> *king . . .*
>
> *and*
> *his*
> *lands. . . .*
>
> *This*
> *day*
>
> I
> *begin*
>
> *to put*
> *fear and dread*
>
> *of you*
>
> *into*
> *every*
> *nation*
>
> *under*
> *heaven. . . .*

~

For Christians, another way is appointed (though, let it be added, in shame and confusion of spirit, that other way is long neglected and ignored):

> If anything seems to stand at opposite poles, it is the ethic of the holy war and the teaching of Jesus on nonviolence. I speak of "teaching" with some diffidence; what Jesus said really cannot be condensed or synthesized into a set of rules. If his sayings are turned into rules, the rules contradict each other.
>
> They (the sayings) rather communicate an ethos, a spirit, which treats each situation as unique, yet itself remains the same. I realize this is vague and unsatisfactory. . . .
>
> When I am urged that Jesus did accept violence when he drove the money-changers out of the temple with cords, I go along with the effort to make rules; I point out that Jesus would have encouraged the sending of an American expeditionary force to Viet Nam, if the force had been armed with whips of cords.
>
> John McKenzie,
> *The Old Testament without Illusion*

~

And what to make of the "anathema" or "curse" or "holy war"? The Jerusalem Bible offers a labyrinthine justification:

> By the anathema, the conqueror is sworn to complete his conquest, by sacrificing all to the divinity; everything is passed through fire and blood.
>
> In this barbarous practice, a religious sense of the absolute rights of God is expressed in the pitiless destruction of the conquered.
>
> Yet the anathema plays its provisory role in the beginnings of the . . . Revelation. The "curse" inculcates in the people of God — in accord with the rudimentary moral categories which they share with the ancient Orient — the transcendence of Jawe; later, this will be manifested as a universal, merciful Paternity.

And more, in a like tone. From the same source we are also assured that ". . . the severe law of the anathema also knew relief, particularly in Deuteronomy."

One turns to the references cited (c. 3, v. 7), and is astonished. "Relief" means this: cattle were spared for booty.

And (c. 20, vv. 13ff.) the "relief" includes sparing women, children, and cattle — likewise given over as booty. Some relief, one thinks — and some exegesis.

~

The ancient slaughter, let it be confessed, leads in due course to the "Christian revelation." In accord (sic?) with which, wars of extermination, sped on by technology, continue to this day. We witness, appalled, the carnage in Afghanistan and Iraq, and, closer at hand, in Palestine-Israel and Lebanon (as the clerical exegetes of the Jerusalem Bible are undoubtedly aware, but choose to ignore).

~

We have suggested, as a clue to the ethos of our text, that a taint of imperial memory, laden with pride of place, spurs the battles on.

(And one cannot but suspect that a like taint lies on the scholars of the Jerusalem Bible — they being non-Jewish residents of Israel, and the tone of their scholarship hardly unaffected by their status. Or vice versa.)

Chapter 3

3:1-22

The passage reeks of blood. One longs for relief, but alas, little is in prospect — except, perhaps, this sorry comfort: the behavior of ancestors is set in bold relief. Thus did the "religious" leaders of the time of Moses behave, as descried by a later time.

That "later time" had no need of religious justification for its wars. The conflicts of Saul, David, and Solomon were driven by purely secular purpose: the achieving — and, later, the consolidating — of empire.

Booty, riches, conquest, forced labor, world markets — these were the prey, both means and end.

~

This is the festival; we will inter hope
with appropriate mourning. Come, my people.
We will celebrate the massacre of the multitudes.
Come, my people. . . .

Mine is the new religion, the new morality.
Mine are the new laws, and a new dogma. . . .

Faiz Ahmed Faiz, "The Tyrant"

~

We have taken note of the logic, the ethos of empire, strongly affecting this version of beginnings. Is not the empire glorious beyond measure — how, then, could its genesis not be holy?

The wilderness years and the Jordan crossing were willed by the god. So went the reasoning — ex post facto, to be sure. Does not a successful outcome imply, from the start, a divine sanction?

And more: "the temple of the Lord," a guarantee of holy beginnings. By the era of Ezekiel, the cry has become a mighty incantation. The god deigns to dwell with us; are not we, then, to be accounted a godly people?

~

Seize the land, then. The god wills it.

In the anathema, booty of whatever kind takes the form of sacrifice, destruction, non-use. Extermination becomes a religious act. It implies ritual purity (whose rules are set down later in our book).

~

We are hardly comforted by the justification.

Still, one thinks — would a close look at the ravages wrought by

23

American (or European) history — even limited to the century just past — would this yield consolation? Hardly.

And this, for the sorry contemporary record:

Washington, October 14, 2001. President Bush forcefully rejected another offer from the Taliban today to begin talks about the surrender of Osama bin Laden, if the United States stopped bombing Afghanistan.

"When I said no negotiations, I meant no negotiations," Mr. Bush told reporters. . . . He added that he was not interested in discussing Mr. bin Laden's innocence or guilt. "We know he's guilty," he said.

The New York Times

3:23-29

The strange mix of this book! Amid the horrors of the anathema, a tender prayer is inserted.

The contrast, one thinks, is deliberate, a moment of literary genius. Moses asks his god, in effect, to undergo a change of heart. Please lift the sentence that lies heavy on me, forbidding my entrance into the Land of Promise!

Is this god, merciless toward others, capable of mercy toward his own? The prayer is heartrending. Mourning, he sees in the mind's eye every detail of "this good land" forbidden him:

Ah,
let me

cross
over

and see
this good
land

beyond
the Jordan,

this fine
hill country,

and
the
Lebanon.

Shall Moses be deprived of so great a prize, won at such cost? The interminable wanderings. Waiting beyond them, the goodly land, the "blue remembered hills," like an alluring dream, infinitely desirable — and forbidden.

This god of favorites? Beware. Even you, Moses, beware.

$\sim$

In due time a response is issued. Mournfully, Moses reports it to the people. Thumbs down: "The LORD was angry with me on your account [that puzzle again], and would not hear me."

No change, not the slightest. The condemnation stands:

You
shall
not

cross
this
Jordan.

A slight concession. Moses may climb Mount Nebo in the Pisgah foothills, and from there view the Land of Promise. He may look

to
the west

and
to
the north,

to
the south

and
to
the
east.

His eye may turn in any direction. It is all his to view, to admire —
and to mourn. How cruel this litany, every point of the compass outspread, a seamless garment of beauty and beneficence. And he may not
don it, may not glory in it.

The Admonition

No Gods but One (Ch. 4:1-40)

4:1-14

We come to the heart of Deuteronomy. The law, for all its majesty, for its holy source, is not an end in itself. It is given for the sake of wisdom.

Believers are summoned to be wise, a heartening thought. And these "observances," and the consequent wisdom attained, are a social gift as well as a personal one. For its own thriving, the community of faith clings to its tradition — for the sake also of those deprived of so precious a tradition.

~

Those deprived — who are they? Let us venture this. In biblical times (and our own, by analogy), the deprived are citizens of a superstate, stuck in place. Two dimensions hem them (us) in: a present that is culturally infected, and a future empty of hope.

And the past? It offers little instruction, only illusions of "great ancestry," a kind of force-feeding of national mythology. The truth is denied us. We starve, and are fed hand to mouth.

~

And what of the saints and martyrs, what of the long-tested wisdom of the tradition, offered in liturgy, prayer, and sacrament?

Offered, and refused. Socialized amnesia is the norm. Are not secular sacraments at hand? Plenty, accumulation, idols of greed and violence.

What a meager diet of spirit!

~

For those who will shortly enter the Land of Promise, close instructions are set down: "Observe them [the laws] carefully; thus you will give evidence to the nations of wisdom and intelligence. . . ."

A glint of light, the welcoming humanism of Deuteronomy. The implication is plain. Wisdom by its nature wins all hearts; the nations too will welcome and embrace it.

~

But this lauded wisdom — how is it defined and lived out?

No conflict arises in the text, no intrusive or challenging word. Little, in sum, of the Spartan "wisdom and intelligence" of the prophets. Now and again a wise word of Moses falls from his lips, hinting of a greater wisdom by far, a treasure buried in the womb of the future.

In the time of Moses, wisdom is meager, all but spasmodic. Nonetheless, wait. A stroke of providence, and prophecy will bloom.

The gift will be costly to those favored. Invariably the prophets will endure the fury of rulers. Against such wisdom as dares confront the "system," imperial Israel will issue a fierce challenge.

And, not to be forgotten, the "system" includes the system's deity.

So, another task, and a perilous one. This ambiguous god, who approves and even entices the kings, must be unmasked — and indeed supplanted — by Another. The prophets are great subversives.

~

It is as though, in the joy of arrival in Canaan, the Fall itself were canceled. As though, as though. As though the forty bitter years were no more than a mirage. Was the trek repeatedly shot through with bickering, jealousies, revolt, pain, loss, betrayal, idolatry, punishment from on high, death shadowing the living? Did cravings arise for the seductions and certainties of slavery? Were jealous arrows launched at Moses? Did many among the chosen fall to greed or injustice?

All a near mirage. The achievement stands at center stage. In view of the outcome, massive defaults are accounted, at most, peccadillos.

∼

The bones of the old generation whiten in the desert, sign of the stalled wanderlust of the dead. A new generation has risen, ignorant "of good and evil," a people reborn, a wise people. A kind of second creation? So it would seem.

Wonder of wonders — how did this come to be? How, by what miracle did children of the Fallen escape the Fall? Of this mysterious cleansed stain, this recovery of primal innocence, we are told nothing. Ancestors sinned; death removed them. And their children emerge unscathed from sinful loins.

Our brows knot in furrows. Reason, logic stop short.

Intriguing. Does the god long for the restoring of creation — could that first genetic week of innocence, grievously undone, be reversed?

4:15-20

On Mount Horeb the people heard a voice, but saw no form. Later, that ancient event and its implications chilled, as though in a cosmic shift of weather. The event, the voice were frozen in absolute command. No visible form was to be attributed to the deity, self-revealed as spirit, uncontainable, beyond imagining.

The Promise was bespoken, honored, given over; the precious goal was won.

Here and now, in possession of the land, a vast irony shows face. Undoubted achievement; and danger lurks. The chosen are surrounded by peoples to whom every creature under the sun is literally adorable. So a "formless safeguard" is decreed.

∼

It is of note that we Christians go counter to the command of "no images." We take our chances on a "form of God" (and God, it would seem, must take his/her chances on us!). Chances are taken on the beauty of multiple forms, honoring every culture and tradition under the sun; forms of saints as well, every hue and age and condition and rank, from royal to slave. Images abound; they multiply due, it would seem, to a teeming spirit named in Scripture "holy" and "outpoured" — images of Jesus, of Mary, and of the "cloud of witnesses."

No great claim can be implied here, nor would such befit — quite the opposite. Neither "formally" devout Christians nor Jews of the "form-less One" prove notably obedient when the "statutes and ordinances," here announced as binding, come down to cases.

Such cases! These are the prey of the prophets to come. Their ethic will be as specific and probing as a finger striking a stony breast, a fiery eye searing a shifty gaze. This king, these priests — and these defaults (take note, you great ones trembling in the dock): injustice, usury, contempt, false witness, power-mongering, murder.

And "No Mas!"

~

The contrast is striking: prohibition of images in Israel, and images galore among Christians. And neither tradition guarantees fidelity, whether to the imagined God or to the unimaginable One. We are fickly free, one and all — free to be wicked, or creaturely.

The holy wars of the Hebrew Bible? They are assimilated, seized by later eras, succeeded (and bettered — which is to say, worsened) by crusade, pogrom, holocaust, smart bombs, and sanctions, appetitive seizures, brazen interferences, crooked diplomacy, and lust for markets.

And what of modern Israel and the "prior inhabitants"? The litany of crime is horrendous, as the second intifada roils on: demolition of homes, roadblocks, guarded Bantustans, detention without trial, torture, killing of civilians, of children. And suicide retribution.

Despair on all sides — Christian, Israeli, Palestinian, and now Lebanese. On behalf of each, for blow and counterblow, the gods of war strain to the utmost.

~

Now and again, the sound of a "different drummer." This one, much akin to Thoreau:

> The one who swears, affirms, or otherwise pledges himself to support . . . a compact or constitution (of any government), is just as responsible for every act of injury done in strict conformity thereto, as if he personally committed it. . . .
>
> The army is his army, the navy his navy, . . . the gallows his gallows, the pillory his pillory, . . . the dungeon his dungeon. . . .
>
> When the constitutional majority declare war, it is his war. All the slaughter, rapine, ravages, robbery, destruction, and mischief committed under that declaration, in accord with the laws of war, are his.
>
> Nor can he exculpate himself by pleading that he was one of a strenuous anti-war minority in the government. He was in the government. He had sworn . . . that the majority would have discretionary power to declare war. He tied his hands with that anti-Christian obligation, to stand by the majority in the crimes and abominations inseparable from war.
>
> It is therefore his war, its murders are his murders, its injuries on humanity his injuries. They are committed with his solemn sanction.
>
> There is no escape from this terrible moral responsibility, but by a conscientious withdrawal from such government, and an uncompromising protest against . . . its fundamental creed and constitutional law. . . .
>
> He must cease to be its pledged supporter and approving dependant.
>
> Adin Ballou, quoted in
> *The Advocates of Peace in Antebellum America*

4:21-28

Moses has attained old age. Despite the scald of tears and years, his sight is clear. And his moral clarity shines unimpeded. It is as though, falling short of the goal, he is strangely granted another gift: nearing death, an outsider, he envisions the future of his tribe.

He must warn them: in neglect of the covenant, a dire outcome lurks.

Again he raises an outcry, partly reproof and warning, partly prophecy. And we note the accusation: "Because of you."

Unexplained, the default of the people is evoked once more. It is as though Moses must lay bare a wound mysteriously dealt, perennially bleeding. He cannot heal it; no earthly power can. But he can assuage it to a degree, as though with balm in Gilead; a clear message.

Thus Moses comes to his finest hour. He breathes deep, rises to the stature of an Isaiah or a Jeremiah. Simply, he knows this: The future of his people will be terrible.

The desert years? In comparison with what is to come, these will seem a leisurely Edenic stroll, or a picnic of quail and manna outspread on the savannahs of Canaan.

$\sim$

And let the outcome, too, be set down plain. For the most part, his warning will be ignored. Eventually, the chosen will mime the worst behavior of those who once enslaved them, or of those they displaced in Canaan. The Israelites too will grasp after "silver and gold and chariots." They will be complicit in the greed and violence of Hezekiah and the kings, will fall to worshiping sticks and stones, the "works of their hands."

$\sim$

Exile: the terrible prophecy yields a metaphor. The people will be "scattered among the nations."

But we note a related matter. Prior to the catastrophe there occurred a "scattering" of heart and mind. Murmuring, revolt, or forging of a golden calf — the "nations" were hardly needed for preceptor. Was Aaron not at hand, a chief among the chosen, to contrive a darling doll, an idol — and this, even as the god of the mountain was instructing Moses in the true way?

$\sim$

Moses trembles. His spirit quails at the prospect of a grand work unravelling. He reads the hearts of his people, devious and futile. Boldly he speaks, in prospect of the awful day of idols:

I
call

heaven
and earth

to
witness

against
you.

Why? He sees the entire creation, that image of divine bounty, insulted and pillaged. Nature itself cries out a curse. The day of blessing is canceled.

~

Is Moses not prophesying events often to be repeated? The personal (and the social) falling away, the "scattering" of a culture, its religion gone sour or stale or plain inhuman, its economy favoring the few, its violence pandemic?

We wince; a scene of recognition.

~

Though they dwell in Canaan and grand Jerusalem shines, the chosen are scattered, distracted in spirit. The mores of the nations own them.

The phrase is Isaian:

. . . serving
gods

fashioned
by human hands

out of wood
and stone,

gods
which can neither

see
nor hear,

neither
eat

nor
smell.

This will be true, except (Moses continues) for a remnant:

There
will remain

of you

only
the
smallest
number.

A faithful community? It will be cut to the bone of bare hope. For most, the Promise will fall prone before greed, vain longing and excess, spiritual exile and alienation. This is the dark triumph of Solomon and his kind. Irony of ironies, Israel will create a new Egypt, a social pyramid of stony magnificence and dire misery. Repeat the litany of loss: forced labor, poverty of the many, extravagance and contempt and sanctioned violence. These will bear down and down, a gravity that kills.

Then we shall see the end, the decline and fall, the exile, the elite of Jerusalem whipped like cattle into Babylon.

~

God too — an Exile. The deity of Ezekiel, in utmost disdain, will shake the dust from garments and depart the great temple (10:4ff.).

In the event, the august self-exile, Scripture turns Scripture around. The One who chose and led the long walk to freedom now disclaims and abandons.

In such a world, God too is unwanted, is put to the edge, declared irrelevant "for the duration": the day of the locusts, the night of long swords, the eons of the Fall. Ezekiel saw it. True God refuses to cohabit with idols and idolaters.

4:29

It is the nadir of the Promise.

And perhaps only at that point, a point seemingly of no return — at the bottom, the pit, the dry well into which Jeremiah was flung, in social disaster and personal betrayal, the people enslaved in spirit, lusting after perquisites and bribes, betraying and defrauding — at a dead end, belief and trust may be twice-born.

> *Seek with*
> *all*
> *your heart*
>
> *and*
>
> *all*
> *your*
> *soul.*

Come, sweet relief and renewal. And an end of threat and wrath from on high.

How to explain it? The image of Jeremiah the victim is socialized. In our text, humans are stuck in a dark pocket of denial and despair. They (we) must abide there, helpless.

Wait. Helpless, you can do nothing. Then something, Someone — Moses takes to himself the tenderness of an Isaiah, speaking for God, announcing a new order, a new day:

For a brief moment, I abandoned you,
    but, with great tenderness, I will take you back.

In an outburst of wrath for a moment,
　　I hid my face from you;
but, with enduring love, I take pity on you.

Isaiah 54:7-8

Or Moses expresses the pity of a Jeremiah:

I know well the plans I have for you — plans for your welfare, not
for woe, plans to give you a future full of hope. When you call me,
when you pray to me, I will listen to you. When you look for me,
you will find me. Yes, when you seek me with all your heart, you
will find me with you.

Jeremiah 29:11-14

He offers the heartfelt assurance of an Amos:

Seek me, that you may live. . . .

Amos 5:4

He extends the invitation issued by a Hosea:

In their affliction they shall look for me, saying,
"Come, let us return to God,
who has rent us apart, but who will heal us;
who has struck us, but who will bind our wounds . . .

"As certain as the dawn is her coming.
She will come to us like the rain,
like spring rain that waters the earth."

Hosea 5:15–6:1, 3

And, not to be forgotten, he echoes the Psalmist, and a like, persistent
theme:

Of you my heart speaks,
　　you my glance seeks;
your presence, O God, I seek.
　　Hide not your face from me. . . .

You are my helper.
    Cast me not off. . . .

Though my mother and father forsake me,
    yet will God receive me.

Psalm 27:8-10

4:30-31

The lawgiver and seer is transfigured; his heart opens like a portal on a vast perspective.

After the Promise turns sour and the land is defiled, after the debacle of exile, after, after — then, he urges, look to the end. Time is not our enemy; no, though we mortals have become sworn enemies one of another. Nor is God's final function and name "the One Who Sits in Judgment."

In a bad time, lean on the Promise;

> *Your God*
> *is merciful*
>
> *and will not*
> *abandon*
> *you . . .*
>
> *nor*
> *forget*
> *the*
> *covenant. . . .*

At the end, Love; and "all shall be well."

4:32-40

The Mosaic mood turns positively Jobian. Look forward, he urges. Then look back, to beginnings.

Prophetic Moses breathes deep, and his breath issues in a rainbow, spanning the skies of time itself:

Ask —

from
one

end
of heaven

to
the other —

did
anything

so
great

happen
before?

The question is rhetorical, he knows, and they must come to know.
Look back and back, for wisdom consists in this grasp of beginnings.
    This was the genesis set in place by the god, the foundation block of
all things. Look to the week of creation — more closely, to the day of the
creation of humans. There will you find what I found, a god who speaks
from the midst of fire?

Yahweh,
God

in heaven

as

on
earth.

God and no other.

But who forms the words — (apart from the gift that forms them for our sake) — "I believe"? Who can claim that (s)he habitually says, "God and no other? God, and no other god"?

It is the simplest of faiths, and the most difficult. It is the awakening of heart and mind to the truth — an event assailed and disclaimed and derided by the principalities of world and time.

Beware the dark powers of "this crooked generation." They make war on earth, reaching to high heaven. They are sworn enemies of the God of creation, the God of life. Beware them.

Confess: "God and no other."

PART TWO

EXPOUNDING COVENANT AND LAW

Moses' Second Discourse

The Commandments

The Heart of the Covenant (Chs. 5:1–11:32)

Chapter 5

On to the commandments.

Notable here is an insistent homiletic tone. Obedience is a practical matter; it implies a response, here and now: "Not with our fathers did he make this covenant, but with ourselves, who are alive here this day."

Are the people to prosper? If so, in all details of the law, Yahweh must be obeyed.

And a further, crucial note, and prophetic as well: submission to the law is by no means limited to cultic purity.

At last a balance is struck: each, soul and body of law, is honored. Obedience implies specific duties toward the neighbor.

Another image: the piers of a mighty bridge are laid down. The span will soar, challenging time and gravity, joining the Exodus empire with prophetic ideal and vision.

Winds are contrary; still, the people hear the hum of the cables, test the tensile strength by walking, marvel at the weightless grandeur and staying power.

To please Yahweh: behold, the sum of vocation and dignity. The god has acted mightily on our behalf. Therefore we pledge: no other gods.

Thus monotheism is majestically, momentously proclaimed, and for all time.

～

How history turns on its makers and breakers! The nations — which is to say, ourselves — are summoned to confession and worship of "one God." And yet, with infinite subtlety of invention and concealment the command of "one God, no other gods" is millennially violated!

Our century, let us confess, our wars, our greed, our domestic violence mark the nadir of national apostasy. Confess. We Americans are the spoliators, the idolaters of the technique of death.

∽

As the people of choice face the deity, at times we are told of an all but overwhelming fear. They fear the spontaneous combustion of divine anger, of a hurler of thunderbolts. They fear death, unleashed without warning.

What is to be done? Restive and peevish is the tribe; Moses is urged to mediate. Half-willingly, he accepts the thankless role.

It is to become his heaviest burden, but also his glory.

Chapter 6

6:1-9

"Hear, O Israel: Your God is one."

The prayer is named "Shema"; in it, we are told, Jewish piety comes to rest. And then the great summons — to the heart of the matter: to love.

> *You*
> *shall love*
>
> *your God*
>
> *with all*
> *your heart,*
>
> *with all*
> *your soul,*
>
> *and with*
> *all*

your
strength.

〜

A strict command — to love someone? Strange, on the face of it; and perhaps psychically impossible as well?

Perhaps not. For the great command follows on a prior impulse named grace. We are commanded to love One who has first loved us — more, who has lighted in us the flame of divine life. Thus the command signals a kind of recognition scene. Like knows Like, and is known; like embraces Like, and is embraced. It is the holy in us who knows the Holy. It is the love of God in us that enables love. Like heliotropes, we turn to the Light, toward the God who first named us: "Mine."

〜

I have made up a morning prayer to you
containing with precision everything that most matters.
"According to Thy will" the thing begins.
It took me off and on two days. It does not aim at eloquence. . . .

Unknowable, as I am unknown to my guinea pigs:
how can I "love" you?
I only as far as gratitude and awe
confidently and absolutely go. . . .

Whatever your end may be, accept my amazement.
May I stand until death forever at attention
for any your least instruction or enlightenment.
I even feel sure you will assist me again,
　　Master of insight and beauty.

　　　　　　　　　　　　　John Berryman, excerpt from
　　　　　　　　　　　　　"Eleven Addresses to the Lord"

〜

Do such matters risk whirling up and up, out of sight, becoming wildly abstract? Indeed they do. But the mystics, who tend to whirl up and up, also offer relief. They never quite leave our ken, never strike free from gravity, from the mess and muck of time. Quotidian matters of life anchor them; the needs of the neighbor press in and in. Help, they must help.

In matters literally of life and death, the mystics, including the great prophets, are also great resisters. Notably, a link is forged in fires of tribulation, joining love of God and neighbor to nonviolent public witness.

We name the linkage grace. "Costly grace" in the phrase of Bonhoeffer, who earned the right to name it.

And as often as not, a harsh exaction follows: jail and public scorn. And in the case of Dietrich, loss of life itself. All honor to the theologian, rare, who walked his word, even to the guillotine!

~

Someone must go before, pre-empt, prompt us. Thus does the love of God in us leaven the soul's substance, to bestir and respond. Thus, too, that perplexing "command" to love, implying, inviting, and yes, creating multitudinous images and occasions apt to the heart's response. Thus, on reflection, the puzzling "command" makes magnificent sense.

Open the door to love! Once opened, another door lies beyond, and another. Walk the walk! It is the dynamic of life itself — from love to greater love, from discerning the times aright, to public testing, to wisdom. From lesser to greater intensity, and ever greater.

Human response to the command is often wordless, too deeply felt to sit lightly on the tongue. Silence is its element, unneedful of words, the act standing for itself, its own sublime validation. An apron of bread crumbs tossed to the winds.

~

Love of God, love of neighbor: the primordial command.

One summons to mind, and so gratefully, the nobility, good humor, persistence, and fortitude of our Plowshares friends over these years. In law courts and out, in prisons and out, their motto is something like this: "Serious change, mitigation of public folly and fury, through sacrifice."

Change, mitigation?

This too is taken into account, is admitted: their (our) actions exert no visible leverage on ruinous policies. Of mitigation and change, after more than two decades of effort, of arrests and trials and convictions and jailings — little or nothing. Authorities continue on the High Road of Folly — nuclear weaponry, incursions, bombings, sanctions, depleted uranium scattered abroad, a hellish sowing.

And in 2001, day-and-night bombings of Afghanistan.

As the *Village Voice* cogently notes, Osama bin Laden was "our man in Afghanistan."

> But what people often don't get is that Bin Laden wouldn't exist without the support of the Saudi royal family, the most disgusting conglomeration of slave owners.
>
> We should recall that it was the Pakistani Intelligence that recruited him from the Saudi royal family, to fight against the Soviets, to show the Muslim world that Saudi Arabia was behind the war. . . .
>
> The immediate danger is a protracted war, perhaps with tactical nuclear weapons, against impoverished Afghanis. This could only encourage more terrorist acts. . . .

~

A lawyer writes from the Terre Haute vigil, held during the execution of Raul Garza on June 19, 2001:

> As the protesters started to leave, a reporter asked one middle-aged protester if she thought the vigil and the prayers and the witness made any difference. The woman took a deep breath and answered, in a statement I have not seen printed in any paper:
>
> "This makes the same difference as the actions of those who protested slavery in the years it was still legal. This makes the same difference as the actions of those who resisted Hitler while he was still in power. These actions make the same difference as those who fought against segregation while it was still the law of the land. The death penalty will be abolished. This will help speed the day."
>
> That was inspiring!
>
> Bill Quigley, Loyola Law School, New Orleans

~

As with nuclear weapons, the Plowshares actions "will help speed the day."

Though it seems to go nowhere, Do it. Mime publicly, with blood and hammers, your version of the Great Command; true to the word of Isaiah, beat swords into plowshares.

It is as though a postscript to an old scripture were set down, in the lurid light of the forge of Mars. As though a voice were counseling, "Do your utmost. Speak up."

As though the voice added, "No one will hear!"

As has been said to the great prophets: Speak, act, though no one hears, no one responds. Thus God tested them in fire, stoked and stoked: fires of violence, of no mitigation, of no change or favorable outcome.

Worse: as though God too were foreclosing a human response, evoking only moral deafness: "No one will hear. No good outcome will prevail, however passionately, sacrificially you see it."

These Plowshares folk risk life and limb, boarding warships and bombers and entering nuclear weapons factories. On the weaponry they pour their blood, and with household hammers they symbolically neutralize the deadly technology. They pray, and await the arm of the law.

In court, they face prosecutors and judges by turns splenetic and icy with rage. How dare these breakers and enterers, destructors, anarchists, fanatics, etc., etc.! Every ruse contrived by the law of the land is invoked to silence and cow. No expert testimony is permitted, whether regarding international law or arguments from necessity or moral or religious convictions. Close the Bible, silence consciences, criminalize and convict!

The scene often seems drawn from the film *King of Hearts*. The courts resemble a forensic madhouse, its orderlies lording it over the sane, the friends and families and defendants. In such a "legal" shambles, the outcome is a cliché, preordained. An infant could play prophet here; the defendants will be convicted and jailed.

~

The above tells of an act of love, many times multiplied, in close accord with the Great Command. The "neighbor" thereby cherished includes the children of the world, ecology, creation itself.

All thanks to you, all honor, dear sisters and brothers: you who con-
template such actions in prayer and sound purpose, you awaiting trial.
You who, as the millennium opened, were in prison: Elisabeth, Susan,
Philip, Stephen, Paul. Heart and soul, you obey the Great Command.
Thus you edify the community of faith, and redeem a wicked time.

6:10-12

Quite a passage, quite a message!

Gratuitous ends are proposed, and nobly. Let us not linger over ques-
tionable means. Let us suspend for the present our recollection of ignoble
wars, seizure of lands, death of the innocent, the aiding and abetting on
high of such horrors.

Best to take the splendid rhetoric as symbol of the regime of grace, as
pure gratuity. The theme is like a drumbeat — or the heartbeat of a good
and giving god:

> *. . . the great*
> *and prosperous*
> *cities*
>
> *which you*
> *did not build . . .*
>
> *the houses*
> *full*
>
> *of all kinds*
> *of goods,*
>
> *which you*
> *did not*
> *heap up . . .*
>
> *the wells*
> *you did not dig . . .*
>
> *the*
> *vineyards*

and
olive trees

you
did
not
plant . . .

Partial symbols, to be sure, beautiful as they are, and telling. But hardly sustaining close examination. It is as though a supreme fiction governed the images.

The facts of the case, of course, are other than fiction, and hardly pleasant to eye and nostril. The aforementioned benefits and blessings were simply plucked from their authors and owners and transferred to others. They became the plunder of simple banditry.

The lord of heaven is pleased to create lords of earth, the redoubtable "chosen." The twin powers that conspire, on a vast scale, to break and enter — in effect, to destroy — a flourishing culture.

6:13-25

The discourse continues; ever so gradually an image of the deity is emerging. A zealous and jealous god, in pursuit of honor from his own:

Such
wonders

as
were worked

on your
behalf —

Inform the children of the bounteous providence; drum the theme strongly; let the memory live on and on. Monotheism: I your god, and no other! And a barely concealed threat: do not, in consequence, presume to

put me
to the test,

as you
did

at
Massah.

Bitter waters indeed. Moses must draw them up again and again, these brackish waters of memory. It was there, at the place of the struck rock, that he miscalculated, and the great portal of the Promise closed against him. Lost, once and for all, the grand entrance into Canaan land.

He would die at the portal, this one who endured every mischance, who cherished and mediated and with infinite patience brought others to the crossing and entrance.

He must be accounted a hero, and a tragic one, of the stature of an Oedipus, an Agamemnon or a Prometheus. Missing the mark, dying at the portal — while others, a second generation, are favored of the god.

~

As we have repeatedly seen, the deity is moody, beyond prediction, easily aroused to fury, long in unforgiving. He seeks a human interlocutor, a mediator of his lightnings. But — let that one not indulge in doubt, let him not strike the rock a second time!

The eye of divine jealousy turns in many directions and settles on one, the chosen within the chosen. Concerning whom there lurks a dark suspicion: Will this Moses — prophet, lawgiver, mystic, mediator — prove also an interloper, a supplanter? Will he go too far, aim too high?

Intermittently the god praises and blames, exalts and casts down.

Of old, did the god not seek to nip Moses in the bud of manhood, to slay him by night?

Another decision: At Meribah we shall test him, at the waters.

Tested, found wanting. And great Moses must pay, condignly.

Willy-nilly, the god gives himself away. Much is revealed in this commerce with a sublime human, this treatment (one thinks: this maltreatment) of one who, by the god's own admission, is "my faithful servant."

~

And let it not be doubted: the god places his trust in violence. Armed with this ethos, he enters the lists of time and this world: the whip, the lash, the spasm in the blood. To the chosen, this mandate is issued: Do your worst; I am with you.

From the start, in Egypt, he resolves to prevail over other peoples and their gods. (Over peoples and gods who, one thinks, strangely resemble his chosen, and his majesty. For do not the unchosen and their deities likewise place huge reliance on force of arms?)

~

Do we search in the text for a credible god, an edifying one, a god who favors life and repudiates death? If such is our hope, it must be conceded: Up to the present account, we have not come far on the road to discovery.

~

The contention between foreign gods and our god, their people and the chosen, continues fierce. Yahweh, he of the drawn sword, is resolved on a series of battles, a showdown.

Do numbers of powerful tribes stand in the way of the Promise? He will remove these, all seven of them, with distain and dispatch.

It is as though they were not. And lo, they are not.

~

We are in a privileged position: we know the outcome of all this. Centuries later, prophets will clarify the futility of the tactics: the exterminating wars, the scorched-earth policy.

In sublime presumption they will proceed, Isaiah and Jeremiah and Ezekiel, to instruct the deity and his chosen, to urge upon them another, better mind — nonviolence, nonaggression, the arts of persuasion and good sense.

In heaven as on earth, the mighty are summoned to accountability.

~

Meantime, prior to those healers, the chosen are infected with a generational plague and its accompanying demons — injustice, greed, slack conscience, empty religion.

Shall the prophet then dare instruct the god as well — that he be invited to a change of heart?

The prophets will cry out: How the "nations" have subverted the chosen. "Your people" have ironically been transformed; now they bear the image of the detested, the unchosen.

They take possession of Canaan. Only give them time: they will transform the land, and themselves be transformed. The Land of Promise will become, in effect, an imperial Egypt. The noble covenant will be degraded, distained.

And in time, the "chosen" will be named anew: the "detested." Pagans become the instrument of consequence: Babylon batters at the gates of Jerusalem, and the once holy city falls.

Amid the chaos, the hinge of history turns in its socket. The people of promise are declared redundant, finished with. Ezekiel tells it. The god departs from degenerate temple and its priesthood, long gone in idolatry. In exile, Yahweh will side with a new champion, decreeing Babylonian ascendency, later even bestowing praise and a blessing on King Cyrus.

Chapter 7

7:1-11

We are once more in the backwaters of time. The instruction of the god continues; the people have much to learn and to unlearn.

For the moment, we picture them hearkening closely.

Those seven tribes of Canaan — have no truck with them!

The least gesture of humane exchange is sternly forbidden. Abominated are those peoples. The chosen are to regard them as — subhuman.

For a time, they have been useful to the divinity and the chosen. They have built "great and prosperous cities," of which we have heard backhanded praise, "houses filled with all sorts of goods," "dug wells," planted "vineyards and olive trees."

All this is accomplished, and the anathema descends. The tribes are removed from the earth, their stores and lands seized, dwellings and symbols destroyed.

～

Time for lines from a great poem, a demythologizing one.

> I saw the old god of war stand in a bog between chasm and rockface. . . .
>
> And without shame he talked on and on and presented himself as a great one for order. And he described how everywhere he put barns in order, by emptying them.
>
> And as one throws crumbs to sparrows, he fed poor people with crusts of bread which he had taken away from poor people. . . .
>
> Bertolt Brecht,
"The God of War"

～

The footnotes of the Jerusalem Bible remain uncontestedly pious. Symbols and expressions relative to the "election" are dwelt on with implicit approval. Thus:

> The choice is sealed by covenant, and makes of Israel a holy people.
> This theology of election, so strongly expressed in Deuteronomy, undergirds the entire Hebrew bible. Israel is a people apart, a people of God, consecrated to the deity who has initiated the alliance.
> Israel is his son, the nation of Emmanuel, "God with us."

～

Of ethical issues, of extermination mandated from on high, of forced seizure of goods and land, of brigandage in high place and low — in this curious exegesis, hardly a word.

Likewise, of the quality or appropriateness of such "obedience," or the nature of such a god, not a word.

What to say? Does Christ our Midrash, his countervailing life and death, shed no light on such texts?

7:12-16

An ample blessing, a superabundant love, inundates the existence of the chosen; the cornucopia of creation tips in their favor.

It is as though the Fall were canceled. The world changes course, transformed into a garden of innocence and plenty.

~

And we have a foreshadowing of the Gospel and letter of John. The end nears, and Jesus speaks to his own:

The one
who obeys
My commands

is the one
who loves Me.

And that one
will be beloved
of My Father.

I too
Will love that one,

and will
reveal Myself

to
that
one.

John 14:21

And the community of John responds, paying tribute to the divine initiative:

We have come
to know
and to believe

in the love
God has
for us.

God
is
love.

And the one
who abides
in love

abides
in God

and God

in
that
one.

1 John 4:16

Thus a burning arrow is aimed at the heart of reality. A Christian midrash transfigures the earlier blessing.

∼

Then (v. 16), the summer sky darkens in a flash. The peaceable heart of the god turns to stone. What of those others, the doomed seven tribes? From ample, detailed blessing, to a curse, short and unsweet: "Devour them!"

The scapegoating continues. The status of the favored demands victims. The chosen must take to themselves (or the god must take on their behalf) the role of victimizer.

The decree is written in the stars. It is the scheme of things above — and therefore below. Or so it is written.

~

Let it be insisted: the schema of winners and losers is ethically a void. To our consolation it is also provisory, temporary.

Liken it to a manifesto of the Realm of Necessity, the social contract of the Fallen vs. the Fallen. The system holds firm; each side takes up weapons.

But it must be insisted: the system, together with its military implications, is — provisory. Though it stands as nearly the first chapter, the Fall and its consequence is not the final word of the human adventure.

Nor is the Fall the final judgment, as though we were bereft of all hope. No, there has occurred an intervention of God, for healing and reconciliation. An intervention named Jesus.

~

The Moses story marks a stage on the road of human development. A stage — and a dead end, both. The pilgrims must await further (and better) instruction, must await a prophet, many prophets. These will declare in image and mime — and in confrontation as well, and in consequence accepted: God is not like that. It is you who are like that.

And further: You need not be like that.

And finally, a command, peremptory: Be not like that. God would have you otherwise.

As for the Otherwise God — on a day far distant, we will see how he comports himself in the world: neither as victim nor as executioner. He will open a third way.

~

Time, and time's revenge. A question arises (it will hardly be voiced in Deuteronomy, only later): What if the blessing turns to a curse?

It does turn to a curse; consult the great prophets. In the light of their light, it becomes clear: the chosen and the god of the chosen have a long, dolorous way to traverse. The road is sown with ironies and contradictions (for the present, mercifully concealed).

7:17-24

With a neat rhetorical turn, Yahweh pre-empts a difficulty. It may well be argued (in a forceful monologue) that the surrounding nations are stronger than you; how then shall you prevail?

Response. Remember, the god is at your side; he and you together stand unconquerable. Bestir your memories. Did not the sojourn out of Egypt, with disaster plaguing the powerful and vindicating the powerless, make the point?

Then let confidence flourish; the past is present, the future assured. Winners you have been and shall be!

〜

The god, as has been suggested before, is much concerned with scapegoating. There are enemies; to deal with these adroitly, invincibly, is the proper — perhaps the prime — function of the deity and his earthly cohorts.

〜

Alas, it seems clear that we are hardly finished with celestial violence. Worse is in prospect.

The chosen stand on the cusp of conquest. The road of havocking stretches far as the horizon, far as generations unborn.

Still, all is not lost. We are in an enviable place; we know of the great ones to come. They will announce a far different God, will commend a far different humanity.

The poet, who suffered for his convictions, might be speaking through Jeremiah:

We speak loudly but no one understands us.
We are not surprised

For we are speaking the language
That will be spoken tomorrow.

Horst Bienek

~

There is vast speculation as to seemingly contrary evidence presented here and in Chapter 9, verse 3. Was the conquest rapid or slow? Were the indigenous peoples enslaved — which is to say, in a manner of speaking, were they spared — or were they exterminated?

"Little by little" the land was won; thus goes the word here. And the reason adduced is curious: "lest the wild beasts become too numerous for you." Evidently the god is intent on drastically thinning the tribes of Canaan, in favor of the chosen. But animals? The chosen must deal with these as best they might; he will not interfere, is the word.

~

In a sense, the argument is beside the point. The instruction of the deity is devoid of compassion. This monarch is absolute; he will tolerate no rivals. Whatever the pace of takeover, it implies — and approves — slaughter.

Altogether remarkable, the deity. And equally remarkable the effect on humans of such instincts as he arouses.

Dare we say it? Dark proclivities are latent; he would spur them to action. He envisions a clan absorbed in war and pillage, callous toward the defeated.

~

The Bible is a hard schoolmaster; the Word spares us nothing.

This is implied. Long before the exceedingly small, scarcely audible voice of goodness is heard, we must be brought face to face with the worst — our condition.

~

A question haunts the seeking mind. Today, whom does our god resemble? Do we account ourselves believers in a better God than is here presented, better devotees than these ancestors, more humane, compassionate, athirst for justice?

We must answer with care, even at times remain silent, shamed. Christian history gives any such claim the lie.

To be sure, a better God is offered us, a nonviolent God whose counsel is love of enemies. The One who so instructed, so comported Himself, and so died.

And to what effect this exemplary life and death, one must ask, on disciples, ancient or contemporary?

The Grand Inquisitor raises the question, inevitably. Never mind his cynicism, his self-aggrandizing, the contempt in word and deportment. He places the meek, slain Lamb on scales of worldly judgment. And with an icy eye on worth and weight, finds him a victim, and wanting.

"To what effect?" His question must be raised. The Inquisitor knows something we would rather not know: Christian history is written in blood, in blood exacted in violent rituals of retaliation.

Thus reads the record of two millennia. Our history offers small improvement on Ancient Deuteronomy. If any improvement at all.

The eminent Inquisitor, to put the matter plain (and he is a great one for plain speech), speaks for the ancient bloodthirsty deity. That god is his sole (Christian?) resource.

On Deuteronomy, Judges, Exodus, the illustrious official takes his stand. He stands foursquare in "Christendom." He speaks on behalf of Christian chiefs of state and their paraphernalia of death: warriors, diplomats, security advisers, world traders, police, judges, courts, prisons, interrogators, executioners.

Christ stands before him; it is as though this exalted being were miming Pilate. He concedes not an iota of worth or weight to Christ's bitter example — self-giving unto death.

Of what avail, to whose benefit? he asks. Superseding what or whom in realms of power and might? Changing what imperial behavior? Creative of what saints, heroes, exemplars in high places?

As though, as though. As though, on the brutal evidence summoned by this frosty genius, the way of Christ were a chimera, or obsolete, redundant.

~

It is as though Christians held in one had the story of Deuteronomy, and in the other, the gospel. An interminable debate ensues. Which deity to serve?

Brutally, the Inquisitor gets down to cases. Which god will allow Christian citizens of this or that empire to wage war and prepare for future wars, to create misery in a world of plenty?

Christ is silent. He offers no defense.

Bow then, Christians, to that other god, the god of power and might, the prevailing one. Serve him only.

~

Isn't it odd that in this nation, the majority of the population, Christian adherents, claim to pray to and adore a being who was a prisoner of Roman power, an inmate on the empire's death row, that the one they consider the personification of the creator of the universe was tortured, humiliated, beaten, and crucified on a barren scrap of land, on the imperial periphery at Golgotha, the place of the skull?

That the majority of its inhabitants, called adherents of the crucified god, strenuously support the state's execution of thousands of its imprisoned citizens, that the overwhelming majority of its judges, prosecutors, and lawyers, those who condemn, prosecute, and sell out the condemned, claim to be followers of the fettered, spat upon, naked god? Who are we speaking of — Baal of Babylon, Jupiter of Rome, or Christ of Christendom? . . .

I speak from Pennsylvania's death row, a bright, shining, highly mechanized hell. In this place, a dark temple to fear, an altar of political ambition, death is a campaign poster, a stepping stone to public office. In this space and time, in this dark hour, how many of us are not on death row?

Mumia Abu-Jamal

~

7:25-26

The point is underscored: no rivals, no idols. Yet the point would seem to be also — one god, not many.

Let us suppose the truth of the account as set down — the truth being the self-conscious moral superiority of the god over the gods.

This would seem logically to follow: the god bestows on the chosen a peerless gift, a behavior and a culture morally superior to the indigenous peoples, these idolatrous Canaanites.

Large suppositions, to be sure! Under the barrage of subsequent history, the strong wall of supposition teeters dangerously. We are privy to the outcome. In the Land of Promise, the chosen win stupendous battles and settle in. In time they are mastered by imperial urges. They grow secular and demand a king.

The (mixed) blessing is granted them: a dynasty. And in the way of the world, power accretes and concentrates in royalty and priesthood.

The outcome? Disastrous. Through ineffable Solomon, the priesthood is reduced to an imperial artifact. The priests are owned, entailed, imperial hirelings.

∼

Then the prophets appear, and for the first time in biblical history, a hot critique is underway. A critique of god and king and people, of temple and palace: the entire imperial arrangement called into furious question.

Another image. A dance, a daring ballet is underway on the stage of time. Ecstasy and the quest for a new humanity join hands. The dancers mime the one and the many, those outside are beckoned within, those within are motionless, atremble in a stasis of learning and listening, of revulsion, terror, fleeing; then an embrace — slow, so long withheld.

∼

The prophets assess their era. They are masters and disciples both, of stern Deuteronomic tradition. Their people, they insist, have befouled the original vision: behavior is ungodly, pagan, idolatrous. For all their wealth and glory, the chosen have become prey, captured, captivated, consumed. They languish in the python guts of the world, assimilated to an era of rapacity and violence.

The ironies are crushing. Worse begets worse: the Exodus has come full circle; we end where we began. According to the great ones, Egypt, Babylon, and now Jerusalem lie in the cleft of gigantic disorder.

∼

As for the god of that awful era, what of him? We have seen the mighty, cosmic genesis. Thanks to the prophets, the Deity has gained (though provisionally, one thinks) a capital letter.

The old god of power and might has quietly (or noisily) succumbed. True God is announced, proclaimed, honored.

God is named anew. The unassimilated, transcendent, "over against," the utter (and unutterable) Other, the holy Critic of the unholy, the One who takes vehement sides.

This God declares new favorites — those favored by no one, the "widows and orphans and strangers in the land" — those signs, living, urgent, needy, honored repeatedly in the covenant, seeking vindication and welcome.

∼

It is the likes of Isaiah who, in effect (we speak in tropes; how else?), have helped the god mature, come to adulthood. To this degree: God is revealed as faithful — faithful to all, rather than to a tribal few. Thus the image of God is relieved of projection, obsession, captivation, grows to unheard-of moral grandeur.

This Deity belongs to all. In outlook, decree, passion, and poetry, God much resembles his truthful, clairvoyant, inspired vocalizers, the prophets.

Long vanished into the shadows of folklore are the nagging imperatives and threats, the vengefulness, the exterminating fury of the old god. None of these. All nations are summoned, included, beloved. All are parties to a covenant ample as the circle of creation itself.

And in contrast with a former ideology of conquest and murder, a noble vocation is assigned the "nations." They are summoned to peace-making. Swords are no longer their cursed inheritance and legacy. No; plowshares are their blessed inheritance and legacy.

Which is to say, the socializing and sanctioning of violent death is halted, declared sinful, redundant, foolish. Cherishing of creation is the order of the new day, the restoration.

$\sim$

If nature is the new poor, then the Christian option for the poor and oppressed now includes the natural world. If we are to love our neighbor as ourselves, then the range of neighbors now includes the whale, the monarch butterfly, the local lake — the entire community of life. If the common good requires solidarity with all who suffer, then our compassion extends to suffering human beings and other species caught in patterns of extinction. "Save the rain forest" becomes a concrete moral application of the commandment "Thou shall not kill."

This in turn requires us to realize the deep connections between social injustice and ecological devastation. Ravaging of people and of the land go hand in hand. To be deeply true, prophetic action must not get caught in the trap of pitting social justice issues against issues of ecological health, but must include commitment to ecological wholeness within the struggle for a more just social order. . . . A vision of justice as cosmic justice is the only adequate option.

Elizabeth Johnson, "God's Beloved Creation"

$\sim$

God must also issue a solemn warning to the prophets. In the short run, in their own lifetimes, their phobogenous outpourings will go unheard, and worse: in such a world, they risk scorn, calumny, detention, even death.

And God too must be warned as to the fate of the Holy in such a world. Ezekiel saw it, and his bones trembled. Distressful and relevatory was the scene.

In the sanctuary, "strange gods" wantonly flourished (chap. 8). Idolatry pre-empted worship. Holy Shekinah, The Presence, was supplanted. Nothing for it; the Holy One must flee the abomination.

~

The Holy One wanders the earth in tatters, crowned with thorns. In such a world, Yahweh is named anew: a Job, a suffering servant, an outsider, an exile, unwanted, undocumented — in Flannery O'Connor's words, a "shadowy figure, flitting from tree to tree in the back of the mind. . . ."

From the world he made, the world that fell away, God mournfully, distainfully departs in exile. In such a world it is his true estate, truer than an imperial temple:

> Then the glory of the Lord left the threshold of the temple and rested above the cherubim. These lifted their wings, and I saw them rise from the earth, the wheels rising along with them.
>
> They stood at the entrance gate of the Lord's house, and the glory of the God of Israel was up above them.
>
> Then the cherubim lifted their wings and the wheels went along with them, while up above them was the glory of the God of Israel.
>
> And the glory of the Lord rose from the city and took a stand on the mountain which is to the east of the city.
>
> Ezekiel 10:18-19; 11:22-23

~

How poignant, the Word of God insisting that "the God of Israel" must be shown the door, that God has seceded before the gods.

Can this be a dramatic trope, and a truthful one, concerning the monstrous preferences of us humans?

Chapter 8

8:1-6

The discourse of Moses continues. The great man multiplies threats and goads and reminders of past defaults, a veritable Etna of woes heaped on Olympus! A strange, even self-defeating pedagogy?

The tongue of the prophet is in grand flood. And amid the torrent, we note words of purity and power.

Another image: his tirade all but halts the wild waters. A Red Sea of rhetoric turned around! And the prophet (or his god, or both) grows vatic. Thus, by bread certainly we live; but "not by bread alone!"

Bread alone cannot satisfy the native hungers of the soul — neither the "bread of bitterness" which they perforce must eat in Egypt, nor the bread that might (might not) have been contrived by ingenuity in the wilderness.

Nothing of these. The bread fell, befell; it was pure gift. So the manna is elevated to a sacred sign: it is the word of God, descending as bread on the desert ground. The wanderers eat of it, and grow thoughtful.

The theme is taken up in Wisdom and prophecy; Amos harps on it, as do Nehemiah and Proverbs.

~

And Jesus is at pains to bring the theme once again to the fore. "Not by bread alone!" The scene is the desert of another time. Jesus has undergone forty days of fast. At the end, "He was hungry." The tempter approached, insinuating; "Ecolo, hunger, these stones, your power. . . . Why not turn the stones to bread, thus bringing matters to a satisfactory close: hunger assuaged, power shown forth!"

Abruptly: "No. The bread you propose is mere bread, dead bread — to your stony purpose, inedible as stones." But here is the good Word: the bread is risen (Matt. 4:1-4).

~

And in our story of the desert folk, a contrast, a descent to the quotidian, a light touch of folklore. Where the manna connection was sublime, this is charming:

> *Why, in a matter*
> *of forty years,*
>
> *your clothing*
> *never once*

went
to tatters,

your
feet

never
swelled!

And one thinks, If these small matters were their only troubles . . .

~

A tantalizing text is before us. Would that the entire Exodus story were told in the spirit of this episode, a quite wonderful union of the mystical and the fond and fey. If only this were the whole story, this spiritual cornucopia of a benevolent god — no outsiders stigmatized, no scapegoats, no arrows of anathema!

~

In sum, we long for a different Bible, one cleansed of crime and sin. We long for a different god, a compassionate one.

But would such a word be of benefit to us? And are we ready for such a god, against whose virtue we might well be inclined to weigh our own? Is it not closer to the truth to confess that "such a god" has already walked our world — to what effect, in our own awful times, it is indeed painful to inquire?

A different Bible, a "different god." A longing as well that a different people walk the pages — a different Moses and Aaron and Miriam and their adjutants, each more to our inclination, to our ideal. To our likeness?

~

Alas for longings. For good or ill (both have undoubtedly come to pass), take it or leave it (some heeded, many walked away), this is the only story, these are the only protagonists and antagonists, this is the only god. The only one — for a long, dolorous time being.

Our text is an apparently random collection of episodes, as though blown together by chancy winds of time. Tales and instructions and aphorisms and ferocious images, its humans wild and woolly (its god as well), unpredictable and stormy, dwarfed and noble. Its kings are like a line of Macbeths; their hands reek of blood. They betray and lust and amass booty and play the world's game to the hilt — all the while uttering and enacting a contrary fealty in worship, psalm, and liturgy.

~

The god, too, sets us off-kilter. As we have seen time and again, he is no great improvement over his favorites — in fact, he closely resembles them, morals and all. He is vexing, peevish, a frosted genius apt to murderous tantrums.

~

Too close for comfort, this Bible, too edgy for easy pondering, no handbook of self-improvement, no counter to lust and anger and hatred, with its parade of improbable wild men and women, its unexpected heroism and shocking crime.

Too close for comfort. Close to things as they are, to "the world, the way it goes." Close to ourselves, as we are. The god closely resembling our gods, the ones we long for, fabricate, set at large in the world, pay tribute to.

The Gods of the Millennium
The god of expectations made money like mad, made money like butter in a churn, poured it out like butter over popcorn, on the deserving and covetous alike. For this, the god was blessed and applauded.

And that was a good year.

The god of approximations made the kingdom almost come. Granted, there were brutish wars and mini-wars, major and minor contusions on the world map. There were bombings from the skies and sanctions against expendable children. And at home, a mood of floating discontent and mutterings of "Get the bastards."

Still, by and large the sanctuaries were full, and the preachers preached, and the collections were satisfactory, and the authorities sat upright in pews of the National Cathedral. There, the president mounted a bully pulpit to intone a doctrine of bloody tit for tat. He went respectfully unchallenged.

And that was a good year.

Seated on a bed, a lotus in perfumed water, the god of stillness intoned, "You think; therefore you are. Think, think." So they thought and they thought and they were and they were.

And that was a good year.

The god of Christians staggered uphill, dragging a plank of wood heavy as a plowshare. Like a plowshare, the plank carved a furrow. From the furrow sprang armed warriors, redundant lives, talking skulls, teeth on edge, disconsolate dragons. These were followed by a multitude clothed in blood. And a girl named Cassandra brought up the rear, raving into the wind.

The procession was of small moment, and went all but unnoticed.

Except for this: for money, bully pulpits, prayer wheels, armed warriors — that was a very bad year.

Daniel Berrigan

⌇

Like no other book in the world, this Bible of ours. Unlike other tomes, histories, tragedies, comedies, operas, epics. In this crucial regard, unlike: the hand of God rests on it; the spirit of God broods over it. This we believe. The text transcends itself; it reaches into the soul and marrow of those who ponder it. It evokes faith, demands it, confers it — all three.

The book is alive, a pitch of life and urgency. It draws us in, even as it repels. If we are attentive and grant it serious attention, a shock of recognition strikes. It is finally ourselves who come alive in these pages, our beginnings, our primordial disaster, our present plight. The best and worst of us suffer there, sin there. And — believe it — are redeemed there.

⌇

Careful — this mirror shows the truth. Hours, days, years, a lifetime in its company, and one's hair stands on end, in fear and trembling — and, as well, in hope, fleeting, abiding, vanishing, returning. A hope proffered in no other pages.

Can it be that there is a God who speaks from there to here, from then to now, spanning time and place and culture and touching us in eye and inner ear and heart — today too, awful today?

For Christians, the Hebrew book leans slightly to one side on the shelf, as though expectant, as though waiting. It leans toward another, similarly bound, a "Volume Two," a Further Word.

8:7-10

It is as though Moses were grown starry-eyed, or invoked starry memories of an unspoiled Eden. Truly, the lost past is recovered in the found future. What a land he invites the chosen into! The prophet waxes lyrical: it is all a gift, a superabundance pressed down and flowing over.

The tone is of a First Week of genesis. Canaan is presented as though newly created, pristine, a paradise.

What a contrast to that other landscape recently, scorchingly traversed — that desert of "serpents and scorpions and thirsts."

The myth continues, and grows by exclusion. The Land of Promise is peerless; other lands cannot match it. Metaphors abound, like newborn spring lambs. It is all an "as though." Canaan yields its lineaments only to the imagination — as though the magical land had newly left the hand of the creator, uninhabited, an Eden prior to Adam.

Lo, the chosen enter, awed. The land is given over to them, as though to its first and only stewards.

$\sim$

Fearful is this method, this sweet cheat. The book trembles in our hands. Why? Because the gift is tainted in the giving, the ethos ambiguous and high-handed.

Is the land unentailed, uninhabited? So it is implied.

What a cruel fiction! The land is indeed inhabited and entailed.

Canaan might be thought of as the first "America." Alas, there will come a second, our own, together with a second "ethnic cleansing." On each scene, the ancient and the postmodern, so widely separated, a vicious myth takes hold. It bears a double form, a contrasting analogy. Either there are no prior inhabitants (one myth). Or if such there be (another myth), let them be dispossessed. Or exterminated.

8:11-20

The chosen are not to forget: the divine beneficence is a mutuality, a divine-human commerce. The land is a gift that keeps giving — or it does not. Conditions are attached to the deed of possession, weighty conditions.

According to Moses, the truth of memory is the first stipulation. Remember, remember — where you came from, from what plight and by whose hand you were liberated. Let the memory be constantly renewed, made present in the "anamnesis" of liturgy. Thus you will understand, and constantly renew understanding.

More. If prosperity is to endure, it must be through close adherence to covenant. Otherwise, worldly ways will seize you, assimilate you, body and spirit, to the idols.

Chapter 9

9:1-6

Time is stilled; time holds its breath. We stand at the verge of the Jordan. Ahead lies the New World, golden under the sun, teeming with promise.

Alas, the chosen are shortly given pause. They learn that, once entered, the land conceals, shall one say, a number of complications.

Did prophet Moses, in his ecstatic travelogue, forget something? Ah, now he recalls it, an embarrassment of sorts. This: the land of high promise is not, alas, devoid of population. It is in fact largely inhabited (as, in the account of Exodus, the Hebrew scouts reported, trembling with fear).

Moses dwells on this human wall of resistance:

> *nations*
> *more numerous*
>
> *and stronger*
> *than yourselves. . . .*

their
great cities

fortified

to
the
heavens.

The prophet is a rhetorician of note. He continues, caught in the fine woven net of imagination. The Power That Shall Prevail, the greater glory of Yahweh! The chosen are to know it: the land will pass into their hands through the might of the god and no skill of theirs.

And what of those inhabitants? They are, of course, not informed; but their existence has been written off. Ironic indeed. The Canaanites, unknown to the newcomers, a stone in the shoe of the Grand Entrance, an embarrassment to the Promise — beyond doubt they worship their own gods. And through their deities, are they not granted an assurance much resembling that of the invading force?

Prior possession is a brawny strength. Push coming to shove, under the aegis of their deities, the Canaanites are prepared to battle for a land "teeming with milk and honey."

~

Too bad for them. It is as though a balancing scales stood on the moon, with gravity all but nullified. On the scales where the Great Plan is weighed, the Canaanites count for hardly a featherweight.

"Swiftly" the land will pass to others, as this rhetorical flourish has it.

With difficulty and "step by step," according to a more prudent account (ch. 7, v. 22, as well as Exod. 23:29-30).

~

Now, tardily, we have an admission: a "Canaanite people" exists.

Such being the case, embarrassment arises. How explain the decree of their extinction? What necessity governs it?

The rhetorician is also a moralist, though of a curious bent. Here Moses mentions a charge against one tribe, the Anakim. His words are both abrupt and (one thinks, necessarily) vague. Something akin to "wickedness" or "perversity" is twice invoked.

Meaning what? One theory, more persuasive than others, mentions idolatries. The imputation, on the face of it, is a puzzle. The Anakim, alas for them, have lacked all access to Yahweh. Therefore, on a sound and logical basis, the tribe is free of guilt, their borders closed, their ignorance invincible.

Can it be that the "wickedness" is a somewhat tawdry, tardy afterthought? The imperative of the case, to the mind of the deity and of Moses, is simple and final. The land must be won — at whatever cost, by whatever means.

~

The access of Moses to the deity is impressively close, if puzzling to the moral sense. We have, nicely veiled in pieties, a bizarre interplay of interests and obsessions, human and celestial.

In any case, let the invasion go forward.

9:7-25

The great discourse continues. The chosen are bidden to recall the transgressions in the desert. Episode after episode is set before them. A pedagogy is strongly implied: in memory lies healing, as well as proof against recidivism. Remember, remember, repent anew. And the assembly (and we with them) are treated to a reprise of the most grievous delict of all. Tell it — be ashamed!

At the point and peak of the desert years, when Moses was in close communion with Yahweh on the mountain, the chosen fell away from the god, from one another, from vocation, from the truth of life.

How could it be? They grew weary of awaiting the return of their intercessor, and enlisted Aaron to undertake a vile project. At their behest (remember, remember!) he fashioned a golden calf. And one and all fell to idolatry.

~

Hear it once more! Moses descended the mountain. Horrified, shamed, half-doubting the evidence of his eyes, he encountered a scene of lusty, orgiastic chaos. And in righteous fury, amid the revelers he cast the stone tablets to the ground. Finis. This people is a total loss.

The god, too, witnesses the scene. He rends the heavens asunder, determined to destroy them, every one. Including the chief delinquent, Aaron.

Nothing for it. Moses must placate the grievously offended deity. At wit's end, he undertakes a forty-day fast.

(The fate of Aaron is an interesting addition to the Exodus text, in which Aaron, it is written, walks free of consequence. Here, Moses must make intercession for his brother and the entire tribe.)

~

As for the abominable image, the calf, let it be burned and ground to dust, and the remains flung in a mountain torrent. Exodus, we note, adds a humiliation of note: the people were forced to drink from the stream, polluted by the lees of their idol. A nice, if lowering, touch, and a primitive avoidance technique as well. The faces of delinquents are pushed deep in the evidence of their misbehavior.

9:26-29

The prayer of Moses begs a mitigation of divine wrath. And a long tradition is invoked: Please, look not closely on the perversity of this people. Surely all is not lost; you (and I, Moses) summon exemplars of fidelity, a litany of heroes: Abraham, Isaac, and Jacob. These redeem a perverse generation.

There follows a familiar reasoning, and potent as well: the theme of divine honor is played, evidently to strong effect. This: Only think of it, Yahweh! If condign punishment descends, what will be said in the land from which you freed us? (And let its name be not so much as mentioned.)

Surely, words of contempt, of dishonor. Something like this: Why, all along the god hated these people. He led them forth only to bring them to ruin in the wilderness. Some god, theirs!

Is the god to bear it, a wave of derision from a nation of idolaters? The suggestion, adroitly launched, touches the deity. He yields; the fury abates.

Chapter 10

10:1-5

The first ascent of the mountain ended in disaster: idolatry and the breaking of the tablets.

Moses wins a second chance. Up he goes, bearing a new set of blank tablets. Once again the godly finger inscribes the Tremendous Ten. Bearing the sacred burden, Moses descends, this time to a chastened, attentive throng.

The sacred legacy of tablets will be placed in a box of fine-hewn wood, the "ark of the covenant." The chest and its contents comprise the presence of the One Beyond Imagining.

10:6-9

We have a delicious aside, a priestly intrusion in the text. In the centuries between Exodus and Kings, a strong clerical culture has risen. The Levites (in this tradition often confused with the priestly caste) have their own interests, and nudge them into the scroll.

Their concerns coincide with those of others. A national "search for pure sources" is underway, a sifting of the many strata of the Pentateuch.

∼

In writing (more, in rewriting) history, a problem arises. In many instances, the sources are hardly to be thought objective or free of self-interest. They call to mind the stream into which Moses cast the dust of the idol. The defection of Aaron at Horeb has polluted the waters.

Then, eventually, to the writing. And it is as though we were perusing another analogy of the Sin named Original. Is the bloodline of the chosen tainted from its genesis?

We imagine the perplexity, centuries later. The Levites of Jerusalem, secure in status, must admit that their founding priest was complicit in idolatry, and for his defection paid dearly.

This was one source, one story. The descendants recoiled; the version was judged intolerable, a slander against an unimpeachable ancestor. Not to be borne! Let us purify the source, remove the story of priestly beginnings from the person of Aaron. Even from the place of his death.

Quick, then, a revised version. Aaron died; his son Eleazar was appointed priest. Here, voilà, is our true founder. And let us leave the dead to bury the dead.

∽

The caravan lumbers on and on in the effort named (if named at all) "Salvage the Start of Things." Further and further through time and place they voyage, away from Aaron, from his corpse even, and from his memory.

And with regard to the day or year of his death (so the reasoning goes), let us be deliberately vague. "It was at that time . . ." that we, the sacred Levites (in effect), took our start.

∽

In so touchy a matter, let us be vague — and, as occasion arises, let us be precise.

As to the crucial matter of continuity, on this hangs the priestly credential. Here, let us be as exact as ingenuity may contrive. So: our sacred office continues "even to this day." More: we Levites are effectively set aside from the common lot, the earning of livelihood. We live from the offerings made to Yahweh, whom we serve.

10:12-17

Surely we are offered here the noblest of the Mosaic counsels. Of the words promulgated on the Mountain, this is most often summoned. The point and pith of the ten commands come to this: the love offered God and one another.

There could hardly be revealed a better way. Jesus will declare as much:

> One of the scribes . . . asked him, "Which is the first of all the commandments?"
> Jesus replied, "The first is this. . . . You shall love the Lord your

God with all your heart, with all your soul, with all your mind, and with all your strength. The second is this: You shall love your neighbor as yourself. There is no other commandment greater than these."

Mark 12:28-31

~

The rhetoric of Moses mounts and mounts, as though once more he were ascending in spirit the mystical mountain. Speak aloud; celebrate the grandeur of this god (and the grandeur as well of the seer, his soul pierced with an intuition of the grandeur of god).

The Father (excerpt)
Unmov'd, Thou mov'st the World about;
Unplac't, Within it, or Without;
Unchanged, time-lesse, Time Thou changest;
Th' unstable, Thou, still stable, rangest;
No outward Force, nor inward Fate,
Can Thy drad Essence alterate.

To-day, To-morrow, yester-day,
With Thee are One, and instant aye;
Aye undivided, ended never:
To-day, with Thee, endures for-ever.

Thou, Father, mad'st this mighty Ball;
Of nothing thou created'st All,
After the *Idea* of thy Minde,
Conferring Forme to every kinde.

Thou wert, Thou art, Thou wilt be ever:
And Thine *Elect*, rejectest never.

Josuah Sylvester

~

The word of Moses: Great is our god, not only in himself — he has acted in a great and godly way, in mercy toward you, the chosen. It is as though the age of the prophets were dawning, as though an aureole circled the lawgiver's noble brow.

As though, too, a new mind and heart were aborning in the god. Omitted for the moment is talk of exterminating wars, anathemas, enmities unremitting. Nothing of that, the implacable mind of the "old god."

10:18-22

We had not heard the like before, a description of the action of God in the world; a God who

> *executes*
> *justice*
>
> *for widow*
> *and orphan,*
>
> *and befriends*
> *the alien,*
>
> *feeding*
> *and*
> *clothing*
> *him.*

We approach the words haltingly, with trembling. Do we have here a kind of "incarnation of mutual purpose" — or at least a prelude of such?

God is commending forms of godly behavior. More, is declaring the terms of his/her own godliness, and this in most immediate, carnal fashion. God is approving (and proving), with outstretched hand and succoring will. The needy, the victims — they are the divine prey and the divine passion.

Yahweh, the original "good Samaritan"? The words befit the lips of Christ. They also befit the lips of those not yet born: ourselves. Let us claim them.

∼

The god grows godly, grows toward moral adulthood. And the people of Moses as well — they mature. How grateful we are, witnesses of this mingling in mind and heart, of "who we are" with "what our god looks like."

In the Bible heretofore we had not come on such stories, the commending of compassion, a "new command" verified in action.

We heard again and again the bloody opposite: the god of steely heart, god of battles, protagonist of the fallen, creator of multitudes of "widows and orphans." The god who, moreover, far from cherishing outsiders, urged draconian tactics against them, anathemas and scorched earth.

~

Whence this glimpse of another, far different deity? In verse 19, God urges,

> *So you,*
> *too,*
>
> *must befriend*
> *the alien,*
>
> *for you*
> *were once*
>
> *aliens*
> *yourselves*
>
> *in*
> *the*
> *land*
>
> *of*
> *Egypt.*

In the night and fog, the ominous atmosphere of Exodus and Deuteronomy, the words come as an astonishing relief. Mercy where no mercy had been. Relentlessly, "aliens, strangers, and foreigners" were presented as inferiors, idolaters, a mortal danger to true believers. In consequence, no mercy; let the sword be unsheathed.

~

By hook or by crook, we have landed on another planet, a flourishing world of the spirit. Animated by new words, new realities are commended: compassion, enlargement of heart toward those in need. This is the reward of fidelity, of obedience to "God's commands" heretofore promulgated.

Compassion is placed in its widest context. It is a stigma, an "indelible mark" much resembling the "circumcision of the heart" Moses urges. It changes attitudes; it is visible and tactile, alert toward others, notably toward the despised and excluded.

Changes, to be sure, toward the generous and giving. And the once despised and excluded — what of them? Their hearts too dilate, their hope is aroused. Can it be that they too are valued and cherished?

No one, nothing is left unchanged. This is the miracle wrought by mutuality of heart, warm, willed into being.

~

Compassion is equally the mark of the god who "has no favorites" (suddenly, sic!), who "accepts no bribes," who is "god of gods, lord of lords . . . mighty and awesome. . . ."

And then, how this? The pendulum swings; the god implies that favorites are before him. He is

> *your glory,*
> *your god,*
>
> *who*
> *has done*
> *for you*
>
> *the great*
> *and terrible*
> *things*

your

eyes

have

seen.

~

Surely we have here more than a mere grab bag of declarations and denunciations from on high. Shall we think rather of revelation, breakthrough, birth? The word of a God, newborn, cauled? A word that, wittingly or not, is self-revealing?

Remove the caul! The face astonishes, is beyond imagining. It is wreathed in a smile, a smile that spells hope.

~

We had gotten wearyingly used to the violence of the god, and of violent humans following suit. Then a far different text meets our eyes. It shines like a jewel; something precious has been rescued from the detritus of history, the sorry tale of losers who perish and of winners degraded in the winning.

In commending to his chosen a new outlook and attitude, a way revealed as godly (and this specifically), the "new god" also reveals his heart. Quite literally, he gives himself away.

The process is jagged, uneven. Often the road halts at a cul-de-sac, a momentary dead end. And we pilgrims are brought up short.

Thus an exodus not solely from Egypt, but from the enslaving Fall, is raised to a commanding metaphor.

~

Shortly, alas, the god will revert to form: the fulminations and clash of arms and bloodletting will resume. Still, we have seen something. We must alter or at least defer a conclusion. There may yet be hope for the god — which is to say, hope for ourselves.

And we are left, as often in this unsettling story, with a question. It bursts with implication. Is the god in the process of a "circumcision of heart"? Is he to become less "stiff-necked"? We dare believe so.

Chapter 11

11:1-9

The chosen have seen, at first hand, the "great works." A capital point is made of this. Descendants will have less immediate evidence. At second- or third-hand — or tenth-hand — they will come to know of those saving works through the compassionate works of the community, by word of mouth and liturgical mime.

～

Thus the descendants of the immediate witnesses stand in our shoes — or we in theirs. And for that second or third — or tenth — generation, ourselves — the echoes fade, grow faint. The original saving acts (compassion and healing, noble witnessing and unequivocal teaching, the death and resurrection of Jesus) — how these are apt to fade and pall!

For most, inference will make do, a sermon, a liturgical mimesis, noble forms of hearsay. And now and again, acts of heroism shock our eyes. Someone, a few — a multitude, even — live nobly and die violently: the Guatemalan martyrs, Archbishop Romero, the Jesuits of San Salvador.

Can these heroes help us overcome the pull and tug of culture, routine, appetite, distraction, violence, money-grubbing — a sucking tide that drowns? Do these hold our hearts in ransom, encouraging morally consistent behavior? One prays, one hopes so.

11:10-25

Moses loves Palestine above all other lands. It is as though a lost paradise were being hymned in song and poetry. A land lost to him, a mirage forever receding, this fabled Shangri-la.

As though, as though. The voice of the seer yields to the voice of Yahweh. Now it is the god who sings the beauty of the land, a psalm of its verdant plenitude.

A Song of Songs indeed. Or as though the god took the guise of Adam, singing aloud praise of beloved Eve.

～

Second thoughts succeed first, and correct and refine. We are in the realm of the ecstatic. In the realm also, alas, of a partial truth.

True, the eye of the divinity rests on the wonders of an ecology unspoiled. But off to the side, a blur stains the eye. The landscape is bloodshot. No escape. The Land of Promise is also the Realm of Necessity. There, everything of beauty and allure bears a price. It is heavy, heavy.

Eons before, death claimed the garden of paradise. And now, what is the price of admission to the Land of Promise? Death.

11:26-32

A hard saying: blessing and curse are announced. It is like every setting forth and every arrival: the Great Venture lies under light and darkness.

The blessing would declare that the work is good, is godly. Still, the work is shadowed; dark declivities score the human heart; a curse lurks there.

In a sense, the curse and the blessing dovetail. Each requires the other; each partakes of the other.

The law of the Fall? In our world there is nothing of pure light and unrelieved darkness. Unless confronted by the curse, the blessing implies, whatever exists is good (including ourselves). No Fall, therefore — no fallen creation. This is a religion that easily colludes with worldly crime, a religion devoid of prophecy. Implied is engorging of the beast, cultural self-approval. No argument with the principalities, self-interest, and access to the powers flourishing. Church and state lying together, snug in a marriage bed.

Implied, too, is a god who endorses (or even induces) pride that admits to no boundaries, confesses to no perverse choices.

～

And what of the curse, unmodified and unrelieved? In sum, it would imply that death is in command. Death claims the last word concerning life. Death — with its arsenal of metaphors, methods, weapons, and hatreds, with its willfulness, malice, blindness, duplicity, and greed — would supersede and vanquish life. And the gods of death would ride the world under, the god of life superseded, images of compassion obliterated.

Who could bear it — a cursed world, a cursed history? Who could survive and hope on?

~

The synonym of blessing is the Promise. And the urging that we "choose life," even as we have been chosen for life. This is the hope we walk with. Despite all, steeped in darkness, we walk.

Here lies hope. The curse is provisional; all depends, as is said, on our response to the word of the living God.

~

Together, curse and blessing, and we are sent on our way. The two, mingling in experience, the open hand and the fist, gift and withholding — these express the ambiguity of the human, our predicament and promise. They express also the variety of vocations, the dignity of being "sent." And, above all, the mystery: grace and evil perennially wrestling. Jacob and the dark angel; ourselves and our world.

The Book of the Law

One Nation, One Law, One Lord (Chs. 12:1–26:15)

Chapter 12

We undertake, at some length, proclamation of the "code." The word is plain frustration. How to put a good face on the brutality and brusqueness of the first instruction, demanding as it does the leveling of rival places of worship?

The threat of Canaanite "contamination," as we learn from the books of Judges and Kings, was neither abstract nor remote. It was palpable; it moved like a dark sludge through the veins of biblical history. No one, it appears, no period or political regime or priesthood was immune from the poison.

We trust the word of the prophets, echoing the warning of Moses: Hosea (4:10-19) and Jeremiah (2:20–3:6) issue dire words in this regard.

12:4-7

The solution is typical of the imperial, imperative mind. Accumulate, centralize — behold, the key to ritual purity! (Or so it is implied.) Level the local shrines. Let all worshipers be summoned to Jerusalem.

Hence the stern legislation, which for the most part remained a dead letter — whether under the Judges or under great Solomon and his temple. A majestic rival, the Bethel sanctuary, withstood. And flourished.

12:8-28

The deity pleads somewhat plaintively for the moral improvement of his tribe. At present the people remain lamentably unformed and unreliable:

> *everyone*
> *does*
>
> *as*
> *he*
> *pleases.*

For a time this will be tolerated, but barely. Once settled in the land, the people will be burdened with a different, more rigid moral code.

There follow detailed instructions regarding holocausts, sacrifices, tithes, and free-will offerings, all to be celebrated in that "Jerusalem of the mind," the holy city to come.

12:29-31

And we return to an obsessive, jealously held ground. The deity senses danger, subtle and menacing: pagan rites and their intrusion on belief. He outlines a possible scenario of ruin, and a remedy.

Every contingency must be dealt with. Even supposing the enemy is routed or eliminated, one or another of the chosen might be tempted, ruminating darkly:

> *I*
> *wonder*
>
> *what*
> *their worship*
> *was like?*
>
> *I*
> *would like*
>
> *to*
> *do*

the
same. . . .

But you cannot thus betray Yahweh, who so detests the maleficent practices of the enemy. Why, in worship of their gods, they go so far as to torch their own sons and daughters!

The accusation invites a pause. Do we have here a kind of blindsiding? The deity condemns the alien gods for actions deemed intolerable. Yet their behavior closely resembles his own.

The supreme one fulminates against his rivals. He is also lenient, to the point of absurdity, toward crimes mandated by himself. Thus: once enacted, the anathema will as surely "torch sons and daughters" as the detestable fires of the "idolatrous."

And is the death of vast numbers of innocents to be thought an acceptable holocaust, raised to the honor and glory of the god?

Chapter 13

Threats of death hang heavy in the air: the death of defaulting individuals, the leveling of cities, even of those inhabited by the chosen. "Unforgiving" is the word that rises, as nooks and crannies of guilt are exhaustively probed.

Turn and turn about, the moods. For now, the god will have no part in forgiveness or compassion. Nor will his judgment be quelled by a kind of a priori reverence-at-all-costs. As though true believers were to conclude "After all, ours is the true god," repeatedly, even obsessively self-declared.

His dicta and deeds stand above and beyond any merely mortal "therefore," beyond human figments of logic, beyond even the (surely hypothetical) judging of great Moses.

∼

One day, a few humans will dare to undertake such a chancy, even dangerous task. The prophets will question Yahweh as to the course of the world, the evils that befall the innocent. So will Job.

But this god of Deuteronomy stands beyond questioning, allows no second thoughts. No; it is humans who are judged. The god will probe and question and denounce. He is obsessed, it would seem, with the Fall. Supposing one default, or perhaps another, might possibly . . . Invariably, death is invoked as the solution.

Rid the earth of sinners — expunge the sin! If an entire city has capitulated to idols, level it, destroy all within.

∼

But, but. This:

> Every war
> carries
>
> within
> it
>
> the war
> which
>
> will
> answer
> it.

Käthe Kollwitz

∼

13:6ff.

The mind of the deity is a vane, wildly turning in self-generated storms.

Can this be the god who repeatedly besought love from his people, "heart and soul"? The page darkens. No more talk of love. That theme is expunged; it is as though the word itself had never been coined. As though humans (and the deity) functioned without hearts.

Nothing of those impeding organs! The god yields to another mood, and to a far different task. Now the grimmest of reapers, shod with felt, moves quietly about the world, his scythe describing an ever-widening swath. Thus the blood-ridden commands:

Kill the false prophet.

If required on behalf of ritual purity, kill son, daughter, brother, spouse. (This from the deity who, as we observed, condemned the pagans for like savageries.)

And if, in one of your cities, a Belial arises to lead the chosen astray, let all living beings in that place be declared anathema.

~

We groan in spirit. What a vast distance remains to be trudged on the road toward humanity!

Question: Is the god of the chosen, here delineated, superior to the gods of idolaters? We are hardly convinced.

The waters of time are stirred, moods alter, frowns replace smiles and smiles frowns. We ponder, and ever so slowly learn. The changes are rung twice: in ourselves, in the tricky ways of us humans, our moods — and in the god who is heedful of those moods. And mimics them.

Still, we summon better days, better behaviors, our god's, our own.

An Emmanuel? Until that dawn, we reserve the right to reserve allegiance. Or to deny it outright.

Chapter 14

After an exhaustive listing of clean and unclean animals, the law yields to a measure of compassion. Tithing, or its equivalent, is urged. And every three years, bounty is to be placed aside for the "widow and orphan and stranger."

Another aspect of this stupendous, exasperating god. Ever so slowly, with pain and halting and false starts, we are shouldered toward a better world — or at least urged (but how slowly) into remission of the present awful world. A breathing space. The Year of Jubilee will arrive, the sabbatical year, with its call to renewal of people and earth.

Chapter 15

15:1-6

Every debtor is to be granted a remission — as long as he (sic; presumably only males incur debts) is one of the chosen:

> *Let*
> *there be*
>
> *no*
> *poor*
> *among*
> *you!*

Thus; though later (v. 11) it is admitted with a kind of fatalistic chagrin that

> *Certainly*
> *the poor*
>
> *will not*
> *disappear*
>
> *from*
> *this*
> *land.*

Thus the conflict, the cruel hiatus. The will of the god (newly emerging, to be sure), and the performance of humans.

~

Astonishing, the Promise; perhaps it shocks because it lies so far from experience. Remission of debts is like a pebble cast in a still pond. A blessing is uttered; the pebble falls. Then ripples start outward, an ever larger, visible circle of benefit, both economic and political.

Be compassionate to the poor, and "You will loan to many nations, without borrowing from any; and you will rule over many, and none will rule over you."

~

We are undoubtedly in the era of the "impure motive," an ethic of quid pro quo — hardly an image of grace and gratuity. We are also in the era of winners and losers. Someone, the supposition goes, must "rule over" another. Why not you?

~

The THREE who are first in point of precedence according to politeness: the most infirm, the poorest, and he who does not know the language.

THREE THINGS which, according to politeness, should be prepared for guests: a kind and affectionate reception, a ready and handsome provision, and a friendly conversation.

THREE THINGS which, according to politeness, should not be asked of a guest: where he came from, his worldly condition, and the place of his destination.

THREE THINGS which are indecorous over meat: gossiping, coquetting, and praising or blaming the meat, since it should be received as God sent it.

Excerpt from Early Welsh Precepts

15:7-11

The god ruminates, as is his wont, on the devious ways of humans. Let us suppose this: a believer-turned-casuist refuses or delays an act of compassion. This one turns away from the needy, reminding himself (and perhaps the indigent one as well), "Don't give up; relief is nearing; the year of remission comes." When it arrives, he will open the fist of his purse.

Meantime, he firmly guards it. The hand of a poor man is outstretched. And he goes away, with only this belaboring word: "Be patient. I shall see you when the year turns."

Thus the Jubilee, designed to educate the heart, to urge a compassion that is spontaneous and consistent, is frozen in place.

And what of that non-donor who walks away? He dons the mask of a believer. But his heart is a parched capitalist's, the heart of a trickle-down theorist. Closed fist, parched wadi.

Through such ignoble play-acting, the ethos of the Year of Jubilee is struck dead.

Which is to say, by plain inference every year was to be a jubilee, to invoke compassion. Let the Jubilee year be joined to the years leading up and to the years following. To every year in the calendar.

In our instance, nothing of that. Hearts turn adamant. Time itself is struck dead. Tergiversation, velleity, and outright refusal are inscribed on its dead clock face. An event, a celebration of the human, a drama to catch the conscience — these drift far from original intent. They become equivalent to the Department of Federal Welfare or the National Catholic Charities.

~

What of those six years that precede, and the six that follow?

To pursue our tale. A beggar's hand reaches out. In the frosty eye of the one accosted, this indigent is helpless, hapless — perhaps he is even responsible for his plight, a wastrel or an alcoholic, a ne'er-do-well.

But: Go slow, warns the word of God. Beware those dark, self-justifying ruminations.

And you affluent, tightfisted withholder, be not deceived. The rags conceal an awesome power. It is as though a Jesus figure stood there. He can

cry out

to
the Lord

against
you!

His god takes sides — not, be assured, the side of the stonyhearted.

~

How differently time is reckoned in the episode! As to "that Jubilee relief," its time may be "near" — near, that is, in the calendar of the affluent and selfish. To the needy, the same relief is as distant as a Shangri-la. One is hungry here, now, today. And the affluent promise that tomorrow or next month or next year, manna will fall.

Will the beggar survive to gather it?

~

Each day an elderly African-American street preacher takes up his post on the sidewalk in front of my church in Los Angeles.... One morning he held a prominent hand-lettered sign that stopped me cold. It said: THE CONSCIOUSNESS OF SCARCITY IS THE ROOT OF ALL EVIL.

The idea that scarcity is the root of evil is thought-provoking in itself. But the "consciousness of scarcity"?

Yet I am becoming convinced that this brother evangelist was asserting something fundamental. Teachings around scarcity and abundance lie at the very center of scripture.

These teachings are encapsulated in scripture's Jubilee tradition — a holistic communal discipline that weaves together economic justice, community resource distribution, work, rest, liturgy, and right relationship. . . .

In fact, the socio-economic vision of Jubilee is articulated in rich, varied ways throughout both testaments, threading from Genesis through the Pentateuch and the prophets to the ministry of Jesus and the writings of Paul. Viewed in their entirety, the precepts of Jubilee shape a powerful biblical vision of what I call "Sabbath economics". . . .

Today the crushing burden of indebtedness and profound inequality imprisons more and more people in industrialized and developing nations alike. If our North American churches are to advocate for redistributive justice for the poor, we, like the first-century Corinthians, will have to cease mirroring the dominant culture of global capitalism, with its empty promises of upward mobility and trickle-down wealth. We must turn toward the bibli-

cal vision of Sabbath economics that lie at the heart of the Hebrew
bible, the Jesus tradition, and Paul's pastoral writings. . . .

Ched Myers,
"Balancing Abundance and Need"

15:12-17

The text speaks only of the fate of Hebrews; outsiders will be dealt with
differently.

What then of slaves? A year of freedom is proclaimed in their favor as
well. They are to be freed, and more, rewarded for service, loaded with
the gifts of grateful masters.

Then a stipulation. Suppose a slave grows affectionate, and seeks to
join the family of his former master? The decision is to be honored with a
painful rite of passage. Take an awl in hand and pierce the ear of the slave
— a perpetual sign that he/she belongs to you and yours.

(This calls to mind other symbolic acts of "belonging to another": the
"stamp" placed on the hand of a military recruit under the Caesars. Or,
for Christians, the repudiating sign, the "stigma," the "indelible mark" of
belonging to Christ, to no worldly power, through baptism.)

15:19-23

As to the firstborn of herd and flock: these are beasts of earth, to be sure;
but they are also sacred signs, together with all living beings. And their
dignity redounds to humans as well. Treat all with reverence due. Feast
on their flesh, recalling in song and Scripture the benefits they symbolize,
and the Benefactor as well.

But as you sit to table, beware partaking of the blood. It is a symbol of
life, and must be poured out, in tribute to the Giver of life, free and entire.

~

The heady symbolism falls short, we note, in the matter of enemies —
real, presumed, or declared from on high. These have no part in the honors accorded the firstborn. Quite the opposite. They are signs of — nothing. They cumber the earth. Let them be disposed of. And their blood too;
let it be poured out, wasted.

Awful. Under the iron yoke, the law of enmity, how burdened we are, how disempowered! Across the void of the centuries to these awful days. To this hour and its shame: the war of retribution unleashed in Israel-Palestine, Afghanistan and Iraq.

Chapter 16

16:1-8

As in Leviticus, Exodus, and Numbers, the great feasts of the Pasch and Azymes are here dwelt on. They are central to the turning year.

With a notable difference. Of the foundational texts, only Deuteronomy quotes the deity, insisting that the feasts be celebrated

> *only*
> *at the place*
>
> *which*
> *he chooses*
>
> *as*
> *the dwelling place*
>
> *of*
> *his*
> *name.*

~

Pasch and Azymes (in origin two, not one) are feasts of liberation. As such, they include ritual foods, to be eaten while all within the house stand at the door, poised, as it were, for flight. A dramatic recalling of the departure, hasty and in the dead of night, from slavery in Egypt.

~

Feasts of liberation? Today, who among us would venture that he or she is liberated? Or that he or she has become a liberator of others? We dwell in an encroaching, enslaving culture. We are born unfree; and but for an act of God, we die with hearts and minds entailed. Our Egypt is near at hand. And close and closer: it would claim us, body and soul.

Dark reflections. I summon the women and men who have graced my life. Including the six Prince of Peace Plowshares, who in July 1997 awaited sentencing in a jail in Portland, Maine.

Their crime? On Ash Wednesday of the same year, they boarded a newly commissioned naval destroyer, the *S.S. Sullivan*, in Bath, Maine. They poured their own blood about, and with household hammers worked symbolic damage on the technology of the coffin-ship.

Gratefully I celebrate them, together with those who preceded, and those who, despite all threats and punishments, will follow.

∿

Follow they do. Toward the end of 1999, Susan Crane, Stephen Kelly, S.J., Elizabeth Walz, and my brother Philip symbolically disarmed two A-10 Thunderbolt bombers in Essex, Maryland.

In February of 2000, the four were held, awaiting trial, with their conviction certain, and considerable time in prison to follow.

Free — in prison? Yes. The minds and hearts of our beloved prisoners remain uncluttered and apt. They judge aright, in accord with Scripture, the war crimes of the age. Crimes already wrought, crimes in preparation.

∿

And a like freedom they offer others.

The offer is taken up, with spirit. These "Plowshares actions" have gathered in number and strength, here and abroad. Since 1980, more than seventy such actions have occurred, in the United States, throughout Europe, in Australia and New Zealand.

In a time of all but universal servility before the principalities of death, all honor to them, these women and men of freedom.

16:9-12

Other feasts are instituted; the first, of equal import with the Pasch, is named Pentecost. (Ironically, a like celebration is held by the enemy, the Canaanites. And one marvels: Who is in debt to whom?)

In any case, the Hebrew Pentecost was originally free of the burden of history. It was a single day of rejoicing for the bounty of harvest.

In time, the celebration took on considerable weight. It was as though (at least by conjecture) the Levites disappeared into the text of Deuteronomy, then emerged with the scroll in hand.

Who now owned the text? It had become pre-eminently the book of "the chosen." And among those so favored, the Levitical-priestly caste formed an inner circle, tight as a wound spring.

The priests owned the text; why not proclaim its meaning to all? They proposed, in effect, a motto, clear as it was constricting: "One god, on behalf of one people, in one land, with one cult."

A first necessary step: Moses must be canonized. So it was done. Pentecost too was transformed. Now it marked the anniversary of the giving of the Law to the great intercessor.

16:13-17

The Feast of Tents arose, that charming outdoor festival. Like the original Pentecost, at the start it was simply a harvest feast. For seven days the people dwelt in tents, celebrating the glories of the autumn vineyard, of wine and olive. The deity thus legislated — joy.

Then, a change of moment. Each of the major feasts stipulated that a pilgrimage must be undertaken by "all the males in your midst." Further. The three — the Pasch, Pentecost, and the Feast of Tents — must be celebrated "in a place chosen by God." Code language, of course, for primacy and a single provenance as well: the Jerusalem temple. All local shrines are outlawed. All roads led to . . .

16:18-22

And something more. Who is to say that the god is unconcerned with practical matters?

We have heard before, and shall hear again in the era of prophets, the passionate hope of the deity: Let justice prevail in the world. To this end, a momentous decree is issued: the institution of judges.

The stipulations touching their office are fiercely to the point: just men (sic) rendering just judgment. First, therefore, and above any other credential — personal integrity. For if judicial hands are sullied with lucre, woe betide! Those appointed will inevitably scuttle just judgment:

> *Bribes*
> *blind the eyes*
>
> *of the (once)*
> *wise,*
>
> *and compromise*
> *the cause*
>
> *of*
> *the*
> *just.*

~

Surely this god is endowed with nobility of spirit, his sentiments apt for that time — and any time. He would have humans partake, in this matter of justice, of his own godliness:

> *Judgment*
> *and justice*
> *alone*
>
> *you*
> *shall seek,*
>
> *that you*
> *may*
> *have life,*
>
> *and possess*
> *the land*
>
> *your*
> *god*

will
give
you.

Wonderfully, "life" itself and "the land" are the fruits of justice, as, by implication, death and a parched wilderness are the fruits of injustice.

The unjust are ethically dead. Their works are deadly. And their souls' ecology, could it be made visible, is sere, lunar, profitless.

⁓

The prophets will never tire of ringing changes on the theme. No quest is nearer their hearts. Passion for, search for, tireless exercise of justice — these simply define the human at its noblest. Let violation, contempt, denial of justice prevail — and humanity of the delinquent is scuttled.

Strike the theme hard, strike it home: humanity at our best and worst! Justice above all; injustice be damned!

Judges are to reflect in their decisions the passion of God: that humans deal humanly with one another. Judges show forth in the world a holy regard and compassion for (the theme goes on and on, enlarging as it goes, summoning human woes and weakness) — a regard and compassion for the most vulnerable among us. Precisely these are urgently commended.

Let judges stand with the God who stands with the victim.

⁓

The god intervenes to promulgate the judgeship, which is thus granted the credential of divine origin.

But one day, alas, grievous falling away will mar the auspicious start. Among the chosen, justice will be in scant supply, rare as radium — rare as justice among "the nations." In a sorry, shabby time, judges, the inner circle of the chosen, will itch for bribes.

And when the chosen become an imperial superpower, justice is a lost cause, as the prophets insist. An entirely rightful hope — indeed, a holy one — is crushed; injustice becomes the hallmark of "the chosen." Injustice is mortised in the building blocks of empire: wars, a piratical economy, malfeasant structures, misery within and beyond unsteady borders.

Ezekiel thundered the theme: Injustice among the chosen! It spreads like a miasma, an anthrax of the spirit, an eighth plague — a plague come home, soul and body politic given over to disease of spirit.

~

In effect, structures of injustice banish the God of justice from the imperial precincts. Bellicose polity, forced labor, contempt for "widows and orphans and strangers at the gate," crass societal divisions of rich and poor — these transform the temple of Solomon into a temple of Sodom. Its liturgies caricature a worship that urges justice; its priesthood is reduced to complicity with the criminal and powerful. Everyone, everything is degraded.

Behold the religion of Solomon and weep: it celebrates even as it generates injustice.

Thus the lack, thus the need. Cry it from the city gates, from atop the walls! For this were the chosen singled out, set apart: to do the works of God in the world — works for which the nations are declared radically incapable.

~

In no other area of human life are the chosen bidden so strongly to surpass the Fall. And a tragic default emerges, close: in no other area will the empire so verify and magnify the Fall.

~

Through the god of Deuteronomy a momentous revelation is granted, for the sake of the poor and victimized, languishing under the spleen of the great ones. The chosen are enlisted in the work; through it they will show themselves godly.

The gentile world is an ethical madhouse. Who but the Israelites will speak for the victims, act on their behalf, stand with them?

Alas for the hope of God. Isaiah lived to see the dead end of the institution of judges. He mourned; the noblest human aspirations had gone to rot.

To repair the common default, there must arise, time and again, someone or some few, acute of conscience, often lacking official credentials, untouched by contagion of money or success or ego, intent on righteous behavior, truthful, radiant of soul.

Thus, in due time, a "suffering servant" (perhaps Isaiah himself?) was anointed

> *to*
> *bring*
> *justice*
>
> *to*
> *the*
> *farthest*
> *isles.*

Isaiah 42:4

This, in effect, is the word of the great seer; it is announced before a king, Hezekiah, whose ethic is frayed by tumultuous times. By turns he is terrified, turgid, and wickedly unpredictable (ch. 34).

The word of Isaiah goes fiercely, insistently counter. In sum: "No wars, no exploitation, no vaunting wealth, no destitution."

For so speaking, he will pay up, and dearly — according to one tradition, with his life.

～

Despite all, truth wings its way across the ages. It must be spoken again and again. And at no time more loudly and clearly than in our own.

As these notes were set down, an embattled president played a latter-day Hezekiah; by turns terrified, turgid, and wickedly unpredictable. Waste and betrayal were the vile hallmarks of his regime. Repeatedly, he ordered retaliatory bombings in Sudan, Iraq, and Kosovo.

One knew it from the start of his sordid personal life: at any cost to others, he would contrive a distraction. Let guile weave a rag of credibility over his moral nakedness. Let many innocents die.

And worse is to come.

Chapter 17

17:14-20

A proffer of divine approval of the kingship comes as a surprise. One cannot miss the heavy dose of self-interest. Divine sanction is eminently useful, and nothing is stronger than a fact in place.

The fact is sunk in place, a deeply laid pier: the monarchy long established, the temple foursquare and sumptuous. Religious practice and secular policy walk hand in hand, a marriage of manifest convenience.

One conjures the king's frosty eye, gazing over the shoulder of the scribe, attentive to every nuance and flourish. Matters of permanent record, matters of import; the narrative must be politically correct. Or else.

∼

Which is not to say that the divine instruction, as set down here, is devoid of judgment. Kings labor to cleanse the record — in vain. They too lie under scrutiny of the word of God. Imperial rascals Saul, David, and Solomon are commanded to ponder the scroll

> *all*
> *the days*
>
> *of*
> *their*
> *lives.*

Thus the judgment; they lift their eyes from the text, and see all about them (or fail to see; and this too is accounted a judgment) imperial violation of the commands.

∼

Isaiah and other noble spirits will underscore the words set down, words aimed like a cloud of arrows at the misbehavior of kings. Do not multiply horses and chariots for war; do not amass treasures; do not embrace foreign wives! Such follies, in effect, amount to a "return to Egypt" — and this in more senses than one. The "return" signifies moral and spiritual regression, hunger for the emoluments of slavery, dread of the unknown, of freedom itself.

Ridiculous and tragic at once. Ensconced in Jerusalem, the king, we are told, trades in warhorses with the former oppressor, Egypt. Thus he sets about reversing the laborious path of Exodus.

An abomination, no matter the prosperity or the worldly plaudits descending on the monarchy and the chosen. In effect: You were liberated from Egypt, and you set about creating another Egypt!

The instruction is aware of the besetting sins of the royal line: warmaking, greed, injustice. The kings grow proud and fastidious and draw apart from the common lot. They find devious ways, whether "to right or left," of "getting around the law." One example: a vast chariotry for war, a military budget that would engorge the world.

We note a correction too (though perhaps a minor one) of the scapegoating of women. Here, the taking of "foreign wives" is but one index of falling away; the indictment includes other grave defaults — greed and violence. All to the good.

~

Thus a clue is placed in our hands as well, to the confusion and misery that today make havoc of the human family and the ecology.

Insoluble? Of course, as long as "warhorses, silver and gold" (Isaiah 2:7) are the prey of hearts gone astray; and across the world, cultures of poverty are created and horridly flourish.

Unheeded, despised as it is, the "thou shall not" remains, living, abiding, stern. Awaiting its time.

Chapter 18

18:9-19

As to prophecy, first the ground must be cleared. Works of magic abound among the nations, a constant temptation to the faithful.

Magic of any sort, "incantation, divination, fortune-telling, soothsaying, casting of spells, consulting ghosts or spirits or seeking oracles from the dead. . . ."

Such follies are best understood, one thinks, concretely. Their aim is the enthronement of death, together with the servants of that principality: domination, deceit, vain promises, technological violence, "justice systems" reeking with injustice, hunger and homelessness mortised into the economy, greed and concealment — in sum, the detritus of vanities heaped in a bonfire of time.

~

Of necessity, empires engage in works of magic. These promise the powerful a sure and prosperous passage, through wily turns and twists of polity, pacts and betrayal of pacts.

And when sweet talk fails, try incursions and seizures. In sum, contemn the word of God in favor of a demonology of death.

As in the time of Deuteronomy, so at the present writing.

~

It goes without saying that the "abhorrent practices of those nations" are forbidden in the community of faith.

In place of magic — prophecy.

Thus a parallel institution: together with the kingship (17:15), prophecy (18:15). Twin powers, one thinks. And how consonant with reality. For how are the kings to rule justly if left to their own devices — violent, constricted, self-serving as they invariably prove?

Divine sanction bestows a blessing on king and prophet alike. How canny this god, how aware of the vices of the powerful, inflated with fantasies of virtue. How else are kings to know the truth of their behavior, to become aware of moral limits?

~

As to the gift of prophecy granted Moses, Christians will seize on it as realized fully in Jesus. The theme is elaborated in Peter's address to the multitudes, after he works a healing at the gate (Acts 3:22-26).

And, in a notable diatribe, fiery Stephen will lay claim to the ancient likeness: Moses would have in Jesus his "faithful other" (Acts 7:51-52).

Little matter whether the ancient knew of his analogue-to-come. Jesus would know Moses, and that sufficed. In a momentous epiphany, time collapses. The holy ones commune, contemporary and co-eternal, on the Mount of Transfiguration. There, Jesus "conversed with Moses and Elijah" (Matt. 17:3).

Taking into compassionate account ourselves and our ruinous century, our longing for sacred signs of relief — these towering spirits stand with us.

We believe it: through them, sufficient light is granted for a next step.

Traveler —
there is no path.

Paths
are
made

by
walking.

Antonio Machado

18:20-22

This Yahweh is a great one for rumination and interior dialogue. Thus, to anticipate our questioning, he probes matters that bewilder us or stop us short. Here he offers reflections concerning true and false prophets.

How to know one from the other? Two criteria. The true prophet is faithful to the Yahwist teaching outlined in Chapter 13. And the events he announces come to pass.

∼

Perhaps at this point a review is in order. As suggested before, the text places us within a closed circle. A scribe in government service, or at least royally favored, sets down a kind of "national epic" celebrating the glories of the Davidic-Solomonic empire.

We infer from the text the ethos of the compiler(s). These are in considerable awe of the splendors of temple and state. Their religion is decorous, dogmatic, somewhat parched. In this they resemble their immediate superiors, the priests (or Levites), forming with them a kind of "royal department of religion," overseeing ritual and moral practice.

Need one add that the interests of all — scribe, priest, Levite, king — nicely dovetail?

We note, too, that the scribal story, which is in effect the priestly story, pays little or no heed to prophecy. Though the office receives an official nod in the law, there seems to be no evidence that, as yet, prophets are raising a critical voice.

Now and again a seer will be heard from. But he speaks in accord with common understanding and interests — no harping, please, on social ills; no speaking too stridently. In sum, the interventions are pro forma, and precipitate no serious relief of royal behavior.

No wonder, little or no relief. Emoluments are at stake.

∼

Still, in the book at hand, another tradition intervenes. The northern kingdom also has its say. And a far different word is uttered, a stern one stressing obedience to covenant.

Obedience to covenant? Of course, of course (one almost sees the priest waving the phrase aside). But — does such obedience differ in substance from subservience to the royal will?

It does indeed, insist the northerners. For on occasion, versions of moral and immoral behavior stand in sharp conflict. Is it not true, for example, that in Jerusalem shady matters flourish, justice languishes, special interests intrude? Thus arises a simmering conflict between the severe northern tradition and the powerful (and lax) centrists in Jerusalem.

How clear it is: the believing community (no matter where situated, and including its highly touted royalty) stands in need of constant reminder and exhortation; in need of national days, even years of renewal, rest, reflection. The Sabbath, the Jubilee year, are of paramount import.

∼

In our extant version of "the beginnings," heroes and villains aplenty walk the pages. A moral code is detailed; it binds absolutely, bearing as it does the seal of Moses and underscoring the intervention of Yahweh. The inner group of faithful, the covenanters, receive favor and grace from on high. They form the heart of the divine-human commerce. For renewal and vigor, the tradition rests in their hands.

The circle of tradition is tightly drawn. In the nature of the exchange, many stand outside.

~

Despite rhetoric and reassurance in favor of "widows, orphans, and strangers," Deuteronomic religion must be accounted, for the most part, tribal in rite and ethic. Designed for, and restricted to, one place: Jerusalem.

But not forever. An explosion of universality is not far off. Like it or not (it will hardly be to the liking of the priests), a dawn will arrive. Its blazing sun will be Isaiah, his light piercing the outer dark, far beyond the horizons of the tribe — until "the nations walk in the day."

Chapter 19

19:1-20

Once more, traditions are in apparent collision. A lengthy to-do follows, on matters of crime and punishment. And beware! A "right of private vengeance" is upheld.

On the one hand, the "enemy" is defined. These include some who, claiming prior possession, would cling to the Land of Promise. Such — be they young, old, military, noncombatant, female, ill — are declared anathema.

But, we ask, stopped short — what of compassion, and of prior possession as nine points of the law — even nine points of self-interest? The answer is curt, brutal. Among the conquered, no distinctions or exemptions are permitted. Many of the doomed are able-bodied and could be found useful as slaves — a minimalist morality, surely; but better, one thinks, than a total ethical blank.

Nonetheless, *pereant omnes*. The blank is total, the ethic a void.

~

In strong contrast, the terrifying code, when applied to the tribe, walks gingerly, careful with distinctions. These laws, we are told, are quite nuanced for so early a period; the community appears self-conscious and civilized. To a point.

Thus: there can occur voluntary and involuntary murder. Hence the creation of "cities of refuge," where an involuntary killer can escape the "private vengeance" of a relative of the slain.

~

In the Canaanite wars, as legislated by the deity, no such distinctions hold. Mass killing is approved under law. And predictably, as mayhem proceeds, blood lust takes over. The enemies are reduced to faceless subhumans — they fall to the sword like swine or bullocks.

Were these in prior possession? No matter. They are simply redundant; they impede the divine (sic) purpose. Talk about tribal religion, ethnic cleansing, a circle drawn in blood! By force of such ideology, fair Canaan becomes a freehold of the invaders.

~

What is one to make of verses 7-10, and the "cities of refuge"? Of these, and the law of anathema?

> In the land which your God is giving you in heritage, innocent
> blood will not be shed, and you will not be guilty of bloodshed.

"Innocent blood . . . not be shed"? The irrational shores up a myth. Its logician, the regnant god, must be accounted useful to vile imperial urgings.

19:21

In a single sentence, limits are set to allowable violence (limits applicable, it would seem, only within the tribe).

The notorious, much-maligned "Law of Talion" is bespoken. (An even larger list of lawful amputations and removals, whether of limbs or senses, is given in Exodus 21:23-35: ". . . burn for burn, wound for wound, stripe for stripe.")

Stark, contrary to the above limits, is the history of what might be termed "deregulated vengeance," the latter almost as old as our human tribe. Thus, in Genesis 4:24, Cain slays his brother. And a genealogy of runaway violence is underway. No limits, no taboos are imposed.

An infamous descendant of Cain is named Lamech. He is a cultural antihero of sorts, the first polygamist and the first abusive spouse to walk the Bible. A charming fellow! One all but sees women cowering before his loutish bellowing.

This desert prowler also is high on innovation of a certain kind; he introduces the "blood feud." He has slain "a man for wounding me, and a boy for bruising me." He proposes a mathematics of murder multiplied: "If Cain is avenged sevenfold, truly Lamech seventy-seven fold" (Gen. 4:23-24).

~

Of Cain and his line, nothing more is said in Scripture. And one thinks: What need of more? The bloodline is fallen, the bloody trail easy to follow.

Given time, the way of Cain becomes the way of the nations.

Alas, we have seen the monstrous tribe in action in our lifetime. In our country. The skills of Cain flourish. The savage song of Lamech echoes, a cry of murderous despair, a yell from the mouth of the inferno.

As in the cacophony of bombings and the multiplied deaths of children of Iraq, the slaying of the innocents of East Timor, the slaughter in Afghanistan, Israeli mayhem against the Palestinians. And on and on.

~

Commanded is "a life for a life, an eye for an eye" — which is to say, strict equity between crime and reprisal. Shortly, it becomes clear that the limits are unworkable. Vengeance is never satisfied with an "equal response." Always, those offended insure that a measure be added, another pound of flesh, an "over and above": for one life, two, ten, a hundred, a thousand. . . .

In the original legislation, the lurking power of that "purpose of more" was never quite taken in account. Does something mysterious, something innate, account for the bloody slippage? Perhaps the one offended must simply "prove" something, whether of ego or brawn. Or perhaps witnesses of the original offense are summoned to requite the loss — friends, family. Or a multitude wields monstrous weaponry, an entire nation like a bloodshot eye focused.

In our era, American judgment is pressed close by slavish media, in somewhat this way: "The enemy has mortally offended us; shall the 'leader of the free nations' not vindicate our honor?"

~

In Manhattan, the unthinkable came to pass. The twin towers of commerce fell. Within days, a stupendous military force was assembled and launched: sea, air, land.

A punitive lesson. Before the world, the violated honor of president and people must be vindicated. And in Afghanistan, the skies fell in, invariably on the innocent.

~

Bashert
These words are dedicated to those who died

These words are dedicated to those who died
because they had no love and felt alone in the world
because they were afraid to be alone and tried to stick it out
because they could not ask
because they were shunned
because they were sick and their bodies could not resist the disease
because they played it safe
because they had no connections
because they had no faith
because they felt they did not belong and wanted to die. . . .

because they were loners and liked it . . .

because a card was lost and a number was skipped
because a bed was denied
because a place was filled and no other place was left . . .

Irena Klepfisz

~

Omnideath.

Yet there stands a contrary rhythm, and a powerful one. Dare we conclude that Jesus offers a more exigent God than the deity of Moses, a more consistent God, a superior ethic?

In light of the teaching of Jesus and his suffering godliness, one hesitates to borrow such language. More simply put, and perhaps more accurately, Jesus offers grace, capacity, a new way of regarding the world, its inequities and crimes. Ever so quietly he declares redundant the old god of vengeance. And he surpasses (better, he ignores) the law of strict limits of reprisal.

Which is to say, he urges no reprisal at all, not an iota.

Something new is in the air, a new spirit for the old. Forgiveness and reconciliation become — let us be modest — possible. Possible even to ourselves, who, left to our own resources, might well fall under an ancient curse, the progeny of Cain.

~

This matter of forgiveness, its seriousness, its unprecedented demands, its centrality to the work of Jesus in the world — these demand an extended treatment. In the Gospels they receive it, full and brimming over. The Instruction on the Mountain (Matt. 5:38-48) surpasses the old legislation, in favor of the Spirit spoken of by Ezekiel (36:26ff.).

The teaching of Jesus proposes, creates, crowns a new version of the human. It is verified in him.

~

Throughout our tormented history, forgiveness has proven massively (one almost wrote, genetically) beyond human powers. But through Jesus, as we believe (or do not believe), grace makes a new start possible. The body of humanity, all but terminally afflicted, receives a transfusion from on high. Make the impossible possible, then probable. Make it actual. Behave as though the truth were true.

A stark necessity, in view of our cumbered, disaffected, dis-graced humanity, is this infusion of divine life, of grace. Given the "facts of the

Bible" — including a projected god bent on vengeance and anathema, generations of fervent Cains and Lamechs and their deeds of blood, wars tumbling on wars without end or surcease — in light (or darkness) of our family history, this must be conceded: grace, gift, the succoring and salvaging of God's hand, a sole and crucial resource.

It is as though "bones, dry bones" were empowered to rise and walk abroad.

~

In the Gospels we are offered a different treatment of the same matter. Reconciling can be understood only through hyperbole. Again and again, Peter and the other disciples are urged to forgive whoever does them ill.

On one occasion, Peter brings up the matter. He asked for a number; he must be answered unequivocally. Seven times I am to forgive? No! "Seventy times seven times" (Matt. 18:21ff.).

~

In other words, again and again, times beyond number. Indeed, forgiveness is not apt for numbers at all. It is a matter of the gift that does not give up, the gift of God in us, godliness. For it is godly to forgive.

Summoning as he does a near unimaginable number, Jesus implies this: Always, habitually, no matter the hurt — seek to reconcile. This, though the offense be mortal, though it all but stop the heart — a matter, let us say, of murder, and a murderer to be dealt with.

We have witnessed it, even in violent America. Family survivors of capital crime refuse the legal apparatus of vengeance, the "eye for an eye" ethic. And the healing that follows, the light struck!

~

The state, as we are reminded daily, has its own method of dealing with offenders — as it has methods of dealing with "enemies" abroad. Domestic law: punish capitally. Abroad: bomb, obliterate, thwart, throttle with sanctions, subvert or invade. The tactics reek of death, the innocent falling, tactics that serve only to perpetuate what they purport to stop short.

In nothing is the line more clearly drawn between the ethic of church and state than in this: the naming and punishing of "enemies." Christians are bidden to remove the word from their tongues, from their lexicons. From their hearts. No "enemies."

~

Two matters come to mind: "naming" and "punishing." In the first instance, believers refuse the name attached by the state: "enemies." We refuse to misname those who in the Gospels are named aright: "neighbor," "brother," "sister," "widow," "orphan." We reject the down-putting slurs "undocumented," "illegal," "alien," negating as they do the biblical term: "strangers at the gate."

The right naming, the close contact with Gospel reality, obviates the question of "punishment." Null and void. Punish the neighbor, brother, sister . . . ?

~

Jesus, for his part, does not directly address the state — the Roman state. Hostilities flourish and fester among his people: injustice, seizure of land, burdensome taxes, showcase executions. The "occupying power" is armed and mighty.

His cousin John the Baptizer perished at the hands of "that fox," Herod.

Nonetheless, let official crime run its course, masked as "the law of the land." Jesus' own betrayal and arrest are at hand. Abruptly, with a command, he addresses Peter: "Put down your sword!"

Even as he speaks, a net of vengeance is drawn across his path. He knows it. He turns to disciples — whether of that time or ours. To us who dwell in a world fallen from grace, unity, peaceableness.

His teaching abides, against the grain, scandalous. Have no part in an ethos of vengeance. No capital punishment; no war. Renounce the works of Cain. Let your behavior befit a community reconciled.

The words, one thinks, are commended first to his own soul. His hour came. Official vengeance moved against him. In face of capital execution, his demeanor and word matched to an iota his prior teaching:

Father,
forgive.

They
know
not

what
they
do.

Luke 23:34

Chapter 20

Here, what contrast: a bleak, unequivocally violent passage. It begins with a bald implication. War is taken as a fact of life. Warmaking goes beyond an "if," leaps to a "when." War is simply built into the human condition (built into the divine condition?).

The god knows humans; the god wills war. He prefers us that way, or he is simply resigned to us that way, clinging to the behavior of Cain and Lamech.

And dare one speculate? Is not more at stake than a kind of resignation on high — a shrug, in effect, since we humans are a clutch of crooked arrows?

Dare we speculate that "god and war" form an imperial construct? That the god of the kings is a god of the fallen kings? A god consequent on the Fall, a god who, together with his creation, has entered the Realm of Necessity, and claimed it for his (sic) own?

Hence, our current predicament. The god of war eructates smoke and fog. And his votaries are struck blind. Or are they born blind?

~

War is raised on high like the "sign" offered Constantine. "In hoc signo . . .": "In this sign you shall conquer."

A sign offered? So goes the tale. If so, the sign was grievously misread. Indeed, kings and commanders, in pursuit of their wars, botch such

114

signs as heaven might offer. Could Constantine or his priests have inter-preted the sign truthfully — could they reveal the meaning of the celestial cross, or of the blazing words "In this sign you shall prevail"?

To that cross was nailed a disarmed God, who chose to undergo death rather than inflict it. "Peter, put down your sword!"

Reading the sign aright: "Constantine, put down your sword!"

～

What contrast! In our text, war becomes the acceptable subject of a reve-lation from on high. "When you go out to war . . ." Then, a kind of battle-field manual unrolls from on high. In the first place, the chosen are urged to have no fear, the god is "with you."

An ironic phrase in light of our Midrash, Christ. The same phrase on the tongue of an angel will bring assurance to Mary (Luke 1:28). And the end of the Gospel of Matthew — "I am with you always" (28:20) — offers the early community a like word: a sovereign accompaniment, an aid that fails not.

～

We have taken note of the "eye for an eye" teaching as a limiting factor on violence. Suddenly the same deity offers a warrior people his own in-vincibility as warrant. Do they, one wonders, require such a prod and guarantee?

Of course they do (of course we do!). What stronger impetus than a stirrup cup held to the warrior by the deity of war himself?

～

Still, we are stopped short. Does the boundary of "an eye for an eye" not apply to larger conflicts as well? If so, how is the limitation to be trans-lated in time of war?

In the text, it would seem that the teaching admits of no such bear-ing. The book fairly glories in enmities, divinely ordained. Whom the god has put asunder, let no one attempt to join together!

Because this is accepted, the answer to the first question is a firm "no"; and the second, of course, does not apply.

20:2-4

Timing sets the tone, Davidic time, or Solomonic — though the fiction of the episode would have it otherwise.

A time warp? In any case, our "composition of place" is hardly a pre-Caananite battlefield. It is the imperial city. The tone, the ideology of the episode is unrelievedly triumphal. "Priests and officials" shortly will favor us with homilies and legalities. These form part of, and are party to, the avatar of empire. Crudely put, these officials have debts accruing.

We are well advised to be attentive; indebtedness will color speech and gesture and moral leanings.

~

The scene merits the word *bizarre*. Merits a second word: *contemporary*. In this sense: the god and the paraphernalia of religion are folded into the text, an ominous leaven.

Thus the ideology of the violent god, of the empire, and of the priesthood are fused. God-empire-priesthood. The three are one, unalterably. And no critique is at hand to say nay.

First, the priests step forward. Their task is to offer the ultimate inducement to valorous behavior: a blessing bestowed on the Armed and Ready. The god is with us — we shall prevail!

~

On the induction of religion into armed conflict, the close dovetailing, the divine favor bestowed on sword, cannon, land mine, bomb, nuclear weapon, depleted uranium, militarized space — what need to dwell?

Today as well, the progeny of the priests of Deuteronomy are quick to approve. On the occasion of public crisis, the Reverend Jesse Jackson, the Reverend Billy Graham, or others step forward to counsel the president and to lead in prayer the armed forces.

Other servants of violence are at hand. There are the just-war justifiers, ready to declare that black is white. And the military chaplains, enjoying secular rank and stipend.

~

And in the autumn and winter of 2001-2002, the American Catholic bishops fell in line with the Bush war in Afghanistan. A verbose, abstract document, many times longer than the Sermon on the Mount, was issued. It contained not a single reference to the gospel. And it granted "qualified approval" to the carnage.

The bombing continued. Shortly, a crucial stipulation ("protection of noncombatants") was shattered. The deaths of Afghan citizens — the aged, children, women — multiplied; a month later, the number of deaths surpassed the number killed in New York and Washington on the day of rage.

Christian alertness and simple common sense would have suggested to the bishops something like this: We shall withhold judgment until a delegation of us visits the invaded country, witnesses the fate of noncombatants, and reports home.

Such a step seemed, alas, beyond the capacities of their eminences.

20:5-7

To our text. The task of the "officials" is practical — crucially so. These are appointed to cull the armed forces. Separate sheep from goats? Say rather, lions from lambs.

First, let those depart who admit to unfinished affairs at home. Before engaging the enemy, let them attend to one or another duty.

～

And what of the near-unmentionables (v. 8), those whose knees turn to water at the prospect of killing or being killed, maiming or death, who, in sum, have no heart for the fray? Concerning these, more later.

The "compleat warrior," it is implied, must be of single mind, erotically and ecologically free.

What of those impediments? They are curious, implying as they do human connections — connections which, in view of impending battle, must be sundered.

It is as though the young inductees were candidates for an austere religious order. They no longer can lay claim to a home, a vineyard, a bride. To do battle is the first and sole summons. War, impending death and glory — these require a zen freedom and concentration of mind.

How deal with those impeding connections? Break them; they hinder battle. Thus, the following are declared unfit, by reason of connection (which is to say, distraction):

The recent homeowner. Let him depart to bless his new house, lest he perish in battle and another possess the dwelling.
The planter of a new vineyard who has failed to gather the firstfruits. He must do so, lest he perish and another claim the harvest.
And a third. This one married, without consummating the marriage. Let him do so, lest another supplant him.

~

Praise is reserved for those who stand firm and steady of mind. They are accounted perfectly fit — for killing, for dying. They have rid themselves of whatever impedes the warrior heart, whether it be home, land, or spouse.

Or we note: perhaps the "fit warriors," those ready for battle, admit (to a degree) the above connections. Possibly — indeed, probably — they do. But with a crucial difference: their connections yield to a sound perspective. Their house is not "new"; its potential loss is undistracting. Their vineyards have yielded fruit for years; the year of battle will not mark a first harvest.

And others have "paid the bride price," married, and bedded their wives. Such matters as enjoyment or its loss do not hinder the sword.

Therefore, in effect, the trumpet note gathers a willing herd.

"Leave all. Come follow me." Mars also lays down terms, as austere as those of the God of peace.

~

In an episode of World War I, there passed through a Fench town a battalion of young soldiers, bound for the front. Silent crowds witnessed their passage.

Suddenly, without warning, the marching warriors burst out in a strange, communal bleat, pitiful to the ear. They began "baaing, baaing."

They were a flock of sheep on the road to slaughter, and they knew it.

~

Let us dream. If only the affair in prospect, demanding as it does a strict and single mind, were other than a form of sanctioned murder.

In place of battle, suppose the deity envisioned a communal planting of crops, or a communal house-building, or a wedding feast, with the god acting as host. (We recall the frequent imagery of wedding and banquet in both Testaments.)

Jews or Christians, we could give our hearts fervently to the god who so summoned us.

20:8-9

We return once again to those "officials," keepers of records, charged with including, excluding, coloration, tone, emphasis of the text. Influential indeed, useful, needful. Who besides these will record and endorse the pure, cold resolve of the warrior clan?

~

Then, another matter, a perplexing one. How to deal with those who will come to be known as "conscientious objectors"?

Unwittingly (and, on our part, gratefully), amid war fevers and chills, the text gives itself away. Refuseniks exist even here, amid the tribe of true believers.

The text is laved in contempt. Some among the conscripts are referred to obliquely. They are cowards who threaten the solidarity of the phalanx. The possibility raises a question. It merits a close look:

> *Is anyone*
> *afraid*
> *and disheartened?*
>
> *Let him*
> *return home,*
>
> *lest*
> *the courage*

of
his comrades

flag

like
his
own.

JPS translation

Manifestly, such as these must be denied a part in battle.

Of their numbers we have not a clue. Whether one, a few, or many, they are tarred as "afraid and disheartened" — a predictable warrior's judgment against those to whom killing is repugnant.

How devastating — and how encouraging as well. And how the contempt echoes down the centuries! The resisters are cowards, bearers of a contaminating conscience. Worse: they resist the will of the god. Ungodly.

Have the priests not declaimed, rattling the war drum,

Let not
your courage
falter. . . .

It is
the lord
your god

who
marches

with
you. . . .

Remove the "falterers" from the ranks, lest one or another

make
his brothers

as
fainthearted

as
himself.

NAB

In a time of socialized lunacy, the sane — those who spurn the sword, putting their hands rather to works of peace, who quail at the task of "murder and no questions" — these are stigmatized as outcasts.

~

We must not miss it: a voice cries out from the text, the voice of innocent Abel — or of innocent Christ. A voice, persistent, valiant, sounding above the din of battle. It is the voice of conscience, unenlisted, uncorrupted. A command. Refuse to kill. Hold firm in your resolve, painful as is the cost! In a measure both modest and bold (and its outcome beyond knowing), you invite others to renounce a pervasive insanity. You topple the god of battle where he (sic) would be enthroned: in your heart.

True God. You confer and confess another title: God of peace.

~

There came to our door in the autumn of 1999 a young West Point cadet, a Catholic, scion of a military family. In the clumsy phrase, the youth "had it all": warrior blood, warrior bearing. He was handsome, commanding, disciplined.

Weeks before graduation and commissioning in the armed forces, he walked away.

His story was remarkable. The qualities that made for a "compleat warrior," discipline and thoughtfulness, also made for a quite amazing peacemaker.

He lost everything, and he stood firm. His family washed their hands of him; his chaplain threatened and fulminated.

Marriage was indefinitely postponed. But he was not alone: his fiancée stood with him.

Superiors at West Point summoned him to a ten-hour "hearing."

The Catholic chaplain appeared in military fatigues, prepared to denounce the youth as a renegade with no standing in his church. His father addressed the court by phone from Texas, denouncing his son's betrayal.

Then there appeared a slight hitch in the proceedings. A Catholic bishop, Thomas Gumbleton, had been notified, and arrived on the scene to give testimony.

Before the court session, he sought out the Catholic chaplain of West Point and spoke with him for half an hour. What they discussed was not revealed; but in the course of the entire day, as the kangaroo court droned on, the chaplain sat wordless.

The outcome, at present writing, is pending.

~

Other exemplary spirits speak up in a wicked time:

> August 2001. A group of high school seniors electrified Israeli society by sending an open letter to Prime Minister Sharon saying that they refused to serve in the occupied territories. Drawing attention to Israel's human rights violations in the territories, they said these "do not even achieve their stated goal — increasing the citizens' personal safety." Such safety will be achieved only through "a just peace agreement between the Israel government and the Palestinian people."
>
> In response to their initiative, 430 reservists, combat officers in the Israeli Defense Forces, have since signed their own statement, refusing "to fight this War of the Settlements" and explaining that they "understand now that the price of occupation is the loss of the IDD's human character and the corruption of the entire Israeli society."

20:10-18

Now, on to the conquest of Canaan. Victory, of course, is presupposed. Indeed, how could matters go awry? The remaining question is tactical, of ways and means.

In accord with the will of the god, two sites are under discussion.

First, certain "enemies" dwell at a distance from the land in contention; these offer small risk of contaminating the chosen. To them a choice is offered. Not much of a choice, to be sure: a rock or a hard place.

If they surrender, they are permitted to survive, but only as slaves, objects of "corvee," forced labor. If they choose to resist (and of course are defeated), many will die. The survivors will become the booty of the chosen.

So much for distant tribes, who are not, in any case, the main issue.

As for the tribes of Canaan — following their defeat, extermination is the policy, one demon on the heels of another.

~

Why, we wonder, the different tactic?

The matter is hardly complex. The psyche of the god demands it. He is a jealous deity. And these "throwaway tribes," together with their gods, present a danger to his hegemony.

~

The god of the chosen has a long memory. The chosen have failed him again and again. The golden calf haunts, as does the murmuring in the desert. And what of the tribal memory? Perverse and persistent, it dwells on the odor of a savory stew of Egypt, the "good old days" of slavish plenty.

The god would free them of this encroaching weakness, and sets about doing so. Pre-emptive wars become a crucial tactic. Remove all occasion of default!

~

L'état, c'est moi: "The state, it is myself" — the boast of Solomon's time, and of Israel's royal line.

And what of the wars that continue, centuries after the conquest — how to justify them? They are no longer named "Holy." Nonetheless, they persist. As the empire flourishes, war prevails: a blood-ridden cliché, fruit of a warrior culture. War promises expansion of markets and lands; praise it, then, this "health of the superstate."

Therefore the necessity of a male census, of standing armies and forced labor.

Likewise the god: war is his health, his greater glory.

20:19-20

A strange subject for a time of war. Concerning trees, and a town under siege.

The god is at war, along with his cohorts, rulers, warriors, priests, Levites, and scribes. And a straight-faced example is offered of this: minds slipped of their moorings. To wit: The will of the god is this: Some trees, even if they stand athwart a siege, must be preserved.

The solicitude toward flora raises an ironic question. The question expresses the pith of the matter (a matter of which the questioner seems sublimely ignorant). We have a kind of Oedipus before the sphinx. The question:

> After all, are the trees of the field to be considered human, and therefore also subject to your siege?

A distinction saves all; or so it is implied. Some trees, unlike humans under siege, are useful. One species, a tree that bears fruit, is to be spared; its fruit serves the hungry. Others, proving useful to the siege-works, can be cut down at will.

~

Trees, humans? Trees are to be respected; humans under siege can be cut down. And those who mount the siege enter a like peril.

But more, and worse. Might it happen that some among the besieged surrender and plead for mercy? No matter. Whether the enemy resists or submits, no matter age and sex, they must be cut down. This is the command of the deity; it is absolute.

Such a god we humans created. To our own image. To such depths has the Fall brought us, god and all.

~

The comment in the Jerusalem Bible is mercifully brief as well as morally obtuse:

> This . . . is inspired by the respect for life which characterizes the religions of the time.
>
> But the Israelite legislator introduces a rational distinction between fruit-bearing trees and those from which siege works can be built.

"Respect for life"? Whose life — what life? Such an ethic loses the forest, so to speak, for the trees.

Chapter 21

21:1-9

Curiouser and curiouser. Shall we name the following episode "The Case of the Untraced Murder"? And does the episode connect with the preceding? Perhaps it does.

In any case, we pass from trees respected to enemies decimated. Our scene can be conjured as a kind of mini-battlefield, a rendering of war, down and down to its essence, a single murder. As in the beginning, one thinks, Cain set upon his brother and destroyed him — a primal image of war.

In any case, the geography is important: "If the corpse of a slain man is found lying in the open, in the land which the Lord is giving you to occupy . . ."

A kind of Abel figure lies here; his assailant has fled, unidentified. This at least is evident: the killer is presented as a type of Cain.

What, then, is to be done? There are priests at hand — the same, one concludes, who earlier egged on the warriors. We remember their words, a patrimony of the Fall:

> . . . You
> who are about
>
> to join battle
> against your enemies, . . .

let your hearts
fail not!

Yahweh marches
with you. . . .

The "enemy" was to be defeated, then exterminated.

⁓

In this scene, a compatriot, perhaps a warrior who survived the battle, is brought low — and by one of his own. (And, in contrast, we have no record that a ceremony of expiation followed the anathema.)

In a case of domestic murder, the instruction is exact and detailed. And is not one tempted to credit a most unloving deity with unwonted love? Love for his own, to be sure.

Such ironic connections, such literary skill! A war manual and a manual of expiation are juxtaposed. Hyphenated texts? Uneasy oppositions that tend, despite all, to illumine one another? If a third eye is open, something like the following would flash from the page:

War is murder, and worse. It is fratricide, the murder of brother by brother.

The god commands a policy of extermination and scorched earth. He also marches to war with the chosen. But then, in the face of a hypothetical murder within the tribe, he commands a detailed sacrifice.

In neither case, war or tribal murder, is responsibility assigned, whether on the part of the deity or on the part of humans.

In war policy (in contrast to murder policy), no question of guilt arises. Quite the contrary: huzzahs are raised, accolades proffered, tasks dutifully rewarded.

In the presence of the corpse, the elders are to wash their hands. Implied is an astonishing irony. They are to pronounce this: "Our hands have not shed this blood, and our eyes have seen nothing."

And one thinks, The same words might aptly be placed in the mouth of the deity-liturgist, as he sees-no-evil and washes his hands of the blood of the exterminated.

And what to make of this, as the prayer of the elders proceeds: "Let not the guilt of shedding innocent blood remain amid your people . . ."?

~

In the liturgy as presented, one notes a kind of anti-liturgy. The bizarre rite implies stark contrasts and contradictions, together with an abhorrent tribalism.

The contradictions all but self-combust on the page. It is as though blindness struck an entire society. Every office and dignity — "priest . . . Levite . . . elder . . ." — is summoned to take part in the disconcerting rite.

Favoring a single unknown victim, liturgical niceties abound. In contrast, the universal anathema induces moral numbing.

Sorrowful honors are accorded "one of our own." And as to the enemies — faceless, abstract, despised as they are — let them be damned, literally!

We are left with that.

~

The first time it was reported that our friends were being butchered, there was a cry of horror. Then a hundred were butchered. But when a thousand were butchered and there was no end to the butchery, a blanket of silence spread.

When evildoing comes like falling rain, nobody calls out "Stop!"

When crimes begin to pile up, they become invisible. . . .

Bertolt Brecht,
"When Evil-Doing Comes Falling Like Rain"

~

We are invited to ponder, to draw from the text, as though with a lover's hands, solace for awful days and nights. This and a saving measure of wisdom: to name crime, crime and murder, murder.

Perhaps to summon also, for the sake of those who render our days awful, a measure of compassion.

21:10-14

A female captive is the subject here, and the treatment to be accorded her. (Can it be that in certain instances, only males perish?) Perhaps we are given an example of the "Talion" law, the limit placed on violence. In any case, the captive can be taken to wife. Moreover, she cannot afterward be sold. She cannot be both spouse and source of profit.

What might be the feelings of the captive as to either fate is unknown. Unknown, one concludes, because of no moment.

21:15-21

These several verses begin with dislikes and likes, and the disposition of goods among contenders.

Then on to the example of a son condemned as guilty, whether by family or community. His crime: he is "a gourmet and a drinker." So. He must be stoned to death at the gates of the town. Horrendous.

21:22-23

This event is judged by Christians to be of far weightier moment. It will be seized on and transmitted to a later scripture as a midrash. This: a curse is to be pronounced against one who "dies on a tree."

We note that the one thus punished has been judged guilty of a "capital crime."

(How this would apply to the accusations lodged against Christ is unclear; indeed, the nature of the charges that bring him to death is a matter of immemorial debate.)

A question: Was the original curse applied because of the heinous nature of the crime? Or did the curse follow on pollution of the land through the presence of a hanging corpse?

Whatever the case, in the death of Christ the curse of the law was applied — with a vengeance.

But the sorry spectacle implies a saving element as well: the curse, lying heavy on the Savior, frees all. Frees humans from a curse that places us perennially among "the Fallen," complicit in works of death.

In their most grievous forms, these must be reckoned acts of war and murder, as dwelt on here (a staple of Deuteronomy and passim in the historical books).

And in a sense hardly less awful, one includes in the "curse" systems of domination, betrayal, and exploitation. To wit (and surely the list is partial, to be amplified by victims worldwide): pentagons, supreme courts and "justice systems," international trade agreements and their seizure of land and labor. Also, world banks, sexist church hierarchies, the "religious right" and the "religious left," Wall Street chills and fevers, police benevolent associations, the FBI and the CIA and like spooks and spies, international cartels, "hostile takeovers," multicorporate piracies, sweatshops, armed guards of properties, "gated communities." And the political and military clones who aid and abet such criminalities.

~

Amid stygian works of darkness, good news, literally, is born. We have been freed of these horrid generational legacies. We have seen the sublime humanity of Christ at work, in word and act. So we are urged in the same direction, giving hand, foot, heart, and mind to the works of life.

~

Deliver me from death, my God,
and give me life. Now you have wound
a rope about me. Harshly bound,
I ask you to release the cord.
See how I die to see you, Lord,
and I am shattered where I lie,
dying because I do not die.

My death will trigger tears in me,
and I shall mourn my life: a day
annihilated by the way
I fail and sin relentlessly.
O Father God, when will it be
that I can say without a lie:
I live because I do not die?

                                        St. John of the Cross

Chapter 22

Legislation touches on rights of possession and property. The rules ring remarkable changes; they seem quite sensitive and humane.

A different mood? Indeed, the atmosphere approaches perilously near tenderness.

A god of tenderness? Is this the divine legislator who also decrees the holy war, the anathema? The question lingers, haunts the text. Which offers little or no light.

Perhaps various traditions are converging, all but colliding.

Or could something else be subtly at work? Is the storyteller hinting at an ethical schizophrenia in believers — their (sane) need of a god of tenderness, their (demented) need of a merciless god?

22:5

A delicious, even hilarious prohibition: the donning of clothing across gender lines is forbidden! Wonderful to think that such delicts existed, and laws attempting to ban them must be contrived.

An intriguing question: Can it be that here and there, a macho warrior is doffing his armor, laying aside the sword, in favor of feminine apparel?

A further irony: the law, as stated, is borrowed from the hated Canaanites.

22:6-7

These verses take into account, if one can so credit, a "mother hen and her eggs or chicks." If one chances on a nest, he may take the eggs or newborn for himself — but not the mother.

In such minuscule matters, the comment of the Jerusalem Bible is wontedly pious and banal: "This is out of respect for motherhood, source of life."

Come now!

Chapter 23

23:1-9

Ancient recriminations die hard — or they stubbornly live on. Thus we have a list of "clean and unclean" tribes surrounding the chosen.

23:10-14

As to defining central and peripheral issues, the laws are curiously constructed. Thus: let it be imagined (and no fantasy, this!) that a war is in prospect, or actually in progress. The Israelite warriors have formed a camp at the war front.

A supposition is in place, like a pier set deep in time. To wit: This is a just war; its righteousness goes without saying.

Under sole scrutiny is the ritual purity of the camp. Soldiers are "rendered unclean" by what are curiously referred to as "nocturnal emissions," occurrences that might be thought fairly normal in males deprived of female relief.

The rule: Those so afflicted must quit the camp until sundown, meantime bathing.

The warriors must also carefully bury their ordure, an instruction that one cannot but approve.

The archaic series ends piously. It appears that the deity will not abide a filthy or disorderly ambiance. If such were to occur, he would depart from the precinct, nose held high: "Your camp must be holy!"

And what of the bloody fray? By every supposition it is accounted . . . holy.

23:15-25

Given a highly imperfect society, laws regarding domestic matters seem sensible, even compassionate. Thus we learn that among the chosen are slaves and slaveholders. What then is to be done — should a runaway slave takes refuge in a welcoming household? Instruction: He is to be protected there — or for that matter, wherever he chooses to dwell. By no means can he be handed over.

~

In verses 19-20, exacting monetary interest from a foreigner is permitted. But not from another Israelite, "that the Lord may bless you in all your undertakings, etc."

So be it.

~

Verses 21-23 offer a clear rule. As to vows — honor them!

~

Another rule in verses 24-25. Passing by the vineyard or harvest of a neighbor, one may pluck grapes or wheat to satisfy hunger. But no more — no putting some aside in view of the morrow. (The rule summons to mind former legislation surrounding the manna in the desert: Gather enough for the day, period.)

Centuries later, disciples of Jesus take advantage of the generous laws as they walk through Galilee on the Sabbath, plucking grain from a field. The bystanding Pharisees carp, and Jesus defends his own (Mark 2:23-28).

Chapter 24

24:1-7

Laws and more laws. One surveys them carefully, hopefully. Will they show forth a deity of compassion?

Here is one. A hand-mill may not be seized as indemnity for debt — not even the "mobile stone" (the upper stone) of such a mill.

The Jerusalem Bible puts it plain: "For that would seize life itself (or 'livelihood') as a pledge."

~

On to a deadly matter: that of "kidnapping an Israelite, and selling him." Apart from the law here set down, we know nothing of the extent of slave trading in the ancient tribe. However, the practice existed, as the law testifies. It is judged an abominable default against the "neighborliness" commended by the Decalogue. It warrants a severe prohibition, sanctioned by the death penalty.

24:10-13

By what right may one claim a forfeit or pledge to recoup the equivalent of a debt? At least the creditor must undergo a slight incommodity: he is forbidden to enter a home on such an errand, must press his claim while standing outside.

And if one holds as pledge the cloak of a poor man? The garment must be returned by sundown, lest night descend on the owner, leaving him sleepless and cold.

24:14-15

For once, a rule that surpasses tribal interests and exemptions. Whether a hired servant be a member of the chosen or not, before sundown he must be paid all wages due. The law presumes, and rightly, that the needs of such a one are pressing; "Otherwise he may invoke Yahweh against you."

24:16

Here, a text of great importance on the matter of individual responsibility. Punishment for crime may not be laid on any but the guilty, not even on a relative of the perpetrator.

Nothing of this, but to each his own. Thus wonderfully anticipating Jeremiah: ". . . through his own fault only shall anyone die" (31:30).

~

Jesus for his part is aroused to fury when this matter of "inherited guilt and punishment" is brought up. It is a fiction, and to his mind, a wicked one; it infects even the understanding of his disciples (John 9:2-3).

The "original sin," it appears, resides in the mind of the beholder, who, coming upon a physically afflicted person, concludes that "this man has sinned, or his ancestors."

The fiction is passed on and on. We have seen its virulence in recent years: it would subject those ill of AIDS to the scrutiny of a punishing god.

Those who so judge are stuck in the empery of death. And from that terrain the God of Jesus, a God of compassion and healing, would have all — even the pharisaical — freed.

24:17-18

It is as though the god suffers conflict within, better part battling against worse. What are we to make of him? He is god of the anathema, and God of the "rights of the foreigner"; god of utmost cruelty, and God of "the widow," whose cloak must not be seized for a pledge.

It is true memory that saves — at least on occasion. (And saves the god as well — on occasion.) Thus the chosen are directly addressed. And it is as though the god were also refreshing his own memories:

> *For*
> *remember,*
>
> *you*
> *were once*
>
> *slaves*
> *in Egypt,*
>
> *and*
> *your God*
>
> *ransomed you*
> *from there;*
>
> *that is*
> *why*
>
> *I*
> *command you*

to observe
this
rule.

A poetic rendering, surely. And for the moment we are reassured and edified. Wonderful!

~

The evidence of holy memories is never quite obliterated, not entirely — though worldly prospering is a powerful amnesiac.

And a question: Is it probable that Jerusalemites in the empire of Solomon, recalling the slavery in Egypt, would open their hearts to the vulnerable and victimized?

(Can one push matters further, knowing that under a similar awful system, many among us Americans benefit to the hilt of the blade?)

Heed the words of Henry David Thoreau:

Those who, while they disapprove of the character and measures of a government, yield to it their allegiance and support, are undoubtedly its most conscientious supporters, and so frequently are the most serious obstacles to reform.

Civil Disobedience

And must one not scrutinize closely the laws of our contemporary system, including laws that protect property and contemn human need? Thoreau again:

It is not desirable to cultivate a respect for the law, so much as for the right. . . . Law never made men a whit more just; and by means of their respect for it, even the well-disposed are daily made the agents of injustice.

And in quest of justice, must one not act against the evil he has come upon?

24:19-22

The rulings here are strikingly heartfelt. The god pleads the cause of the inarticulate and victimized. And the believing community is urged in the same direction: Stand with the abandoned, and thus help them withstand!

The chosen have attained the Land of Promise. They have also learned (perhaps from the tribes they dispossessed?) of an ancient pagan custom. In tribute to the god of the crop or the spirit of the fields, a sheaf or part of the olive or grape harvest was left untouched.

Now a like gesture, its motive changed for the better, is urged. The blessing, the ample harvest, is to reach a wider circle, beyond owners and paid laborers. To the needy, those who stand empty-handed at the edge of plenty, a sheaf of the harvest or a measure of olives and grapes is to be given large-handedly.

And be it further noted: the giving hand stretches out and out. The offering is made to "widows and orphans" — and to the "stranger, the foreigner" as well.

Chapter 25

25:5-12

Various arrangements concerning marriage, death, and remarriage (the famous "law of Levirate") need not detain us long. These are clan laws, designed to ensure that descendants and properties are lodged safely within the bloodline.

Chapter 26

26:12-15

Generosity is underscored as a primary virtue — whether of the god or the community. And so may it be, as then, now.

~

Fittingly, the second discourse concludes with a liturgical prayer, to be repeated every third year, in the time of tithing. Believers are to purge themselves of idolatry; they must declare (and the recital is to be matched by behavior) that they have eaten no "bread of lamentation," a reference, no doubt, to the cult of one or another idol: Baal or Adonis or Tammuz.

This latter, referred to here as "the dead one," perished each year in the scorching droughts of July, and was reborn when the rains came. He was honored widely, we are told, even in Roman times.

∼

A concluding instruction (26:16-19) — somewhat redundant, one thinks — concerning the strict terms that bring social prospering. Thus: Keep the commands and ordinances, etc., and I will bless you. Otherwise, ruin will follow.

Surely we have seen the "otherwise," the dire outcome of reneging. Then and now.

3

The Covenant Proclaimed and Renewed (Chs. 27:1–29:1)

Chapter 27

27:1-10

Not only is the law to be observed ad litteram; it is to be publicly inscribed. Thus hearts and eyes are enlisted in tasks of obedience. Further, let an altar be raised, constructed of undressed stones — a nice touch. Nature is respected in the form it left the creative hand.

And finally, another public discourse: this one is a joint venture of Moses and "the Levite-priests." The gist: This day, the day of the proclamation of covenant, you have become a holy people, a people of the god.

27:11-26

Once the tribe has passed over Jordan, blessings are to be uttered atop Mount Gerizim, curses atop Mount Ebal.

Strangely, the words to be uttered go unrecorded. Were they omitted because such blessings were well-known, attached as they were to close observance of the law? In any case, the blessings are to be uttered by the "important tribes," the curses by the less important, beginning with the disputed Reuben. (He, it will be remembered, sponsored the "lesser evil" in the story of his brother Joseph. The same Reuben was accused by his father of incest.)

～

Jesus will take up the curse genre thunderously in Matthew 23:13-36.

～

138

The note of compassion, never quite stilled, is heard again in verse 18: ac-
cursed is one who sets a blind man on the wrong way. And again, more
strongly in verse 19,

> *Cursed*
> *be one*
>
> *who violates*
> *the rights*
>
> *of foreigner,*
> *widow,*
>
> *and*
> *orphan. . . .*

These are classical figures of deprivation — and more. Signs of the
holy amid the chosen, they are to be held in close compassion.

We note once more — we are forced to note — the discrepant god(s)
of the text. The one who compassionates, as above; and the one who creates, through the anathema, corpses. And among the survivors, those of
utmost misery, multitudes of "widows and orphans."

Does a radical uncertainty lurk in the human heart, a question —
which god for ourselves?

Canny author! It is left to us.

∼

Confusion, questions — perhaps our own; these are implied throughout
the text. Who is this "god of our beginnings"? How did he regard our people, enslaved as we once were? By what means did he lead us forth? What
was the fate of the tribes of Canaan, and how did we come to possess the
land? In his interventions, did the god appeal to the best or to the worst in
us? Throughout the story, were justice and compassion the rule of behavior — or were these often scuttled, in heaven as on earth?

∼

A grim anomaly. On the record, engraved in the text for eyes of generations, is this god of double intent: the god of utmost cruelty, and the god
of a mothering face.

Eventually, the texts will come to clarity in the revelation of a moth-
ering God, the God of an unqualified "Yes" — the God of the prophets.
And for us Christians, in the resounding "Yes" of Christ, celebrated by
Paul:

> *Jesus*
> *Christ . . .*
>
> *was*
> *not*
>
> *alternately*
> *"Yes"*
> *and "No."*
>
> *He*
> *was*
> *never*
>
> *anything*
> *but*
> *"Yes."*
>
> 2 Corinthians 1:19

In him, through him, a final word will be spoken concerning the
moral physiognomy of God. Again and again, Christ summons a Father-
Mother of mercy and compassion, One who excludes no one, who is disarmed and nonviolent. And the witness, the messenger, is himself, the
vulnerable One, who will choose to give his life rather than take life.

Need it be said, in this century riven with violence — we have yet to
absorb that ineffaceable Icon. From the date of his appearance in the
world, the blows, the scorn rain down. The holy One cannot be borne
with.

Yet the truth remains. How blessed we are. That Word is literally "of
God." He has taken flesh, has "dwelt among us" (John 1:14).

And
all

the
people

will
say,

"Amen!"

Chapter 28

28:1-14

Vast blessings follow, bestowed on every aspect of human life, and on the ecology as well. The benefits (v. 7) include, as one could darkly surmise, conquest of "enemies."

Who these enemies might be, whether present or future, is a matter, it would seem, for the god to decide. Are the chosen for the moment ignorant of who is to be vanquished? Let them fear not; they will be opportunely enlightened!

Let us venture this clue: The "enemy" is any tribe or army who impedes the designs of the omnipotent warrior.

∼

The Jerusalem Bible is pleased to enlighten us — tardily, as might be thought:

Jawe is also a warrior God [sic].
An ancient Hebrew book, now lost, is named "the book of the wars of Jawe."

We take note: a capital letter is bestowed on the god by the commentator.

~

The blessings, as well as the implied threats, continue apace. It is as though neither the god nor Moses can rid himself of a primordial suspicion. Divine-human commerce will flourish only if the exchange is laced with rewards and punishments.

The god and his prophet, after all, must cope with a tribe notorious for immaturity, capriciousness, changeful moods, the itch of rebellion. Faith and trust blow hot and cold, evanescent as spring weather.

~

A question: Does the atavism, the morality of carrot and stick — does this originate with the tribe, or with the god?

Let this be ventured: Until the age of prophets, everyone concerned in our story is — stuck.

Giants of valor and clairvoyance, Isaiah and Jeremiah must help bring a new mind and heart to birth. How else shall the deity and the chosen break free of reliance on the sword?

The prophets must help the god come of age — a stupendous undertaking, and rife with danger. Through them, God will declare a new way, a new program for humans, set free (at least in principle) from jealousy, tribalism, and wanton slaughter.

Thanks to the prophets, God will be the prize of no coterie, the darling of no king. God will be someone starkly different: an opposition Figure, a God who speaks an unwelcome word and stands by it.

At long last, God and humans (a few) will stand opposed to the crimes of the powerful — the violence, greed, and war-making. At long last, God will declare true God — unowned, unentailed, transcending human default, bending before no bribes, no loss or gain of devotees.

~

What a relief! The prophets will reveal a useless God, a God who cannot be put to vile uses, who disdains the patronage of the principalities, refuses the beck and call of the powers of this world.

What a word, how longed for — and how tardily spoken. Solemnly:

My
ways

are
not

your
ways.

Six monosyllables — and they sum up volumes in the glossary of mystics and hermits and prophets and martyrs. The "Via Negativa," the crucial word, purifying — and preliminary as well. Before the ways of God may penetrate the heart, the "useful gods" must be exorcised, banished.

∼

Under a striking image, Jesus speaks of the exorcism — forcefully, shockingly, as a forced entry, a "binding" and "overpowering." It is as though, indeed, the act, overtly illegal, was performed by him. Notably, three of the four Evangelists record the parable. We quote Luke 11:21-22 (par. Matt. 12:29; Mark 3:27):

When a strong man,
fully armed,

guards
his courtyard,

his possessions
go undisturbed.

But when someone
stronger than he

comes
and overpowers him,

such
a one

carries off
the arms
on which
he was relying,

and
divides

the
spoils.

In sum, an image of the dynamics of the Incarnation. Immanuel will enjoy no easy sojourn in a hypothetical Eden. God must tread the stony ground of inequity, scorn, and rejection.

Inevitably, he will confront a larcenous household, guarded, claimed, and occupied by contrary powers: a tribe of "true believers" in — death.

"Overpowers him," "divides the spoils." Conventional pieties? Hardly. The work of God is starkly otherwise. Possession is, all said, nine points of the law. And dispossession — how many points?

Nonetheless, dispossession, "overpowering . . . dividing" are underway.

∼

To our present text, and the changes to come.

A series of blazing epiphanies will mark the birth of new humanity. A burning coal will be put to the lips of Isaiah. Jeremiah will mime the public woe, and be humiliated and punished for his daring. Ezekiel will tell of the temple long gone in idolatry, as a scornful deity departs the precincts. A vision of the "Human One" will be granted Daniel. And so on.

Until these blazing disclosures, small moral progress can be claimed, whether in god or in people. On earth as in heaven, a horrid routine of "war as usual" will prevail.

The god and the human tribe are bound to a wheel of Ixion or a chariot of Mars. The god is both prize and captive of the imperial succession.

∼

History is a nightmare.

Rabbi Abraham Heschel

~

And what of ourselves? The question is inevitable. That feckless tribe of nomads is our ancestry; we bear their features. And more. We bear their burden: If an Intervention from on high be denied us (it is not denied), they and we stand under a curse. The past is future, stuck, blank, blood-ridden. History is an interminable rake's progress, absurd and vicious, begetting gods of dark desire, the gods we serve — and deserve.

The gods we are served by, in mutual shame and enslavement.

28:15-66

Until the Gift is given. Until then, like Beckett characters, we are sunk in the unsavory stew of the "curses" elaborated in these verses.

We ponder closely; we taste the pain. This is our own story. The words fall like a sevenfold plague, potent, enticing, degrading. They haunt us; they are the voice of the gods of our own day.

First, promises are launched, blessings — of a kind.

Strange. They seem to contain their own opposite, the curses to follow. Of what value is a promise like this?

> If you obey the voice of Yahweh . . . the god will place you above all nations of earth. . . .

A Faustian promise, an ambiguous blessing. It seems designed to dupe, to confuse our human sense. In the estimate of the deity, is the reign of Solomon to be accounted a blessing or a curse, an apogee or a nadir?

Such blessings! They imply both promise and threat; they nudge humans into hostilities — and worse. They entice the "enemy" as well — to move against and destroy the chosen.

~

Thus far have we come — not far at all, hardly surpassing the original Fall. It is as though the ancient page of Beginnings were followed immediately by this awful one, so akin are the two.

145

The images conjure human life as a monstrous bear pit or battlefield, a game of conscienceless winners and losers — and the devil take the hindmost. A horrid anti-Scripture, really.

～

Let this be admitted as well, and dwelt upon; the pondering be medicinal. The curses speak unyieldingly of our own day: the gods we lust after, the behavior that wins the laurel, the loot, the accolade. Images so accurate, so relentless. If we are capable of shame, they humiliate.

Mute, we stand there, as in a scene of recognition. This is the bad news, the prelude, necessary and relentless, to the Good News.

Also implied, though scarcely mentioned, is another, far different behavior. Such words and acts as risk all, and often as not, lose all. Such acts and words as bring the conscientious ("no false gods before me") to scorn and prison, torture and disappearance.

～

This is the good news:

> *The*
> *Word*
>
> *was*
> *made*
> *flesh*
>
> *and*
> *dwelt*
>
> *among*
> *us.*

John 1:14

And the Gift is all but lost, despised, sabotaged, in imperial misadventuring. In a firestorm of hell.

All said, this humanity of ours has not greatly surpassed the diagno-

146

sis of our current Deuteronomic chapter. It reads like a skilled medical chart — our social biography. Our pathology.

∼

A strange mix, these curses and blessings. Let us turn the text about and about, and see what emerges.

Something like this: If you remain faithful to the god, to this image of contrariety and contrast (much resembling your own schizophrenic soul), then all manner of benefits will follow. Nature will benignly serve; enemies will yield; you will rule supreme.

If, however, you are unfaithful to the will of the god, disaster will befall — body, soul, society. Your nation will be utterly defeated, "an object of horror" in the world. Animals and crops will fail; the cosmology will be destroyed. And so on.

One asks: Would not a responsible exegesis dwell on the pastoral implications here?

Alas, the curse-blessing theme arouses far different skills, a kind of textual taxidermy. A dead word is made presentable, a mime (and mockery) of a living word.

Our text is in fact "anciently modern": it breathes tradition and today. It concerns ourselves, our culture, our behavior in the world.

For the nonce, let this be our comment: The god would hold his chosen captive to a text which much resembles, in its moral darkness, a dungeon of the psyche. In such a mix of threat and promise, who is free: the kept, the keeper? Or neither?

∼

The chapter is, as suggested, a kind of anti-text; it must be "deconstructed." A midrash is called for. And such is available, by grace of a later Event, and we the (more or less) enlightened latecomers.

By no merit of our own, we are granted knowledge of true God. Therefore, it would seem to follow that we are enabled to know the idols and their noisome tactics. And this knowledge is hardly inert or abstract.

It is to our shame that we know the idols. Know them? They are welcomed, brought indoors, cosseted, sheltered, fed, bedded. In them, with

147

them, through them, appetites are satiated, skills refined, vile initiatives honed.

∾

This god of Chapter 28 must be accounted . . . an idol. Promises and threats, "toil and trouble," drawn out and detailed.

The idol, moreover, is socialized, a mix of "I" and "we" bespoken by demons. He is the dark, undifferentiated coupling that one day will assault Jesus.

The mood is manic-depressive; the fevers and chills of a culture of death swing us aloft and down, dizzy with promise and threat, reward and punishment.

∾

Can it be that there exists a better, steadier way? There does.

Let us be as positive as the times allow. Let us take the chapter as a long, dolorous exercise in accountability. No crime but is noted and scored. The terrible words are aimed, like a storm of arrows, straight at "the first earthly power of all."

This generation of North Americans, or even the next, may not see the terrible maledictions descend. Or we may. Or, as of September 11, 2001, we may already have seen their fiery first act.

And what the end will be, neither war-blessing church nor warring state can tell. Only this: "They will alight on you and your descendants as a sign and a wonder, for all time" (28:46).

For those with eyes to see, the arrows are already launched. And the first victims are the leaders.

One after the other, on the day of their accession to power, or before, in the brutal scramble for the prize, in money-grubbing and a chaotic war of images, politicians are struck blind. This is the first sign of the Empery of Arrows.

The president of the United States, whatever his name or political inclination or skills or affluence, is struck blind. So are the advisers and cabinet members, beginning with the eminence charged with something known as "national security." So is the newly created, ominous "homeland czar." So, too, another charged with "affairs of state." Also the vast majority of senators and congress people.

~

A second sign of the empery: The leaders are blinded, and they claim sight. Genetically, one thinks, they are incapable of seeing the criminal implication of their deeds. They are skilled in such decisions as bring, inevitably, death in their wake — death repeated and multiplied, as required by the idols named "national defense," "economic prospering," and "American interests."

~

The signs, let it be insisted, are irrevocable. No matter who leads the superstate, drawn from whatever party, adhering to whatever religion — the system lays claim, enervates, engorges. The president, his debts coming due, his policies sad, shiftless, stale, or belligerent, antic, contemptuous of international law or the American constitution — he is immaterial to the course of events. Except to move those events along more and more speedily.

The idols named money, international cartels, trade agreements, "justice systems" with their paraphernalia of racist judges, death rows, "three strikes out," and, privy to every decision, the chief principality, the military — these are the prime movers of what Archbishop Romero characterized as the "security state." Our own.

Meantime, under a mesmerizing incantation of "democracy," "open media," "national self-interest," "moral values," "military necessity" — and that unspeakable evasion known as "collateral damage" — the criminal regime prospers.

So in our text do the maledictions. Arrows strike seeing eyes blind.

28:67-68

We have come full circle. Under the petrifying threat of a "return to Egypt," the chapter is recapitulated.

It seems as though everything has changed — everything except human hearts. Providential events fade to chimeras, faith and trust yield to magical incantation and liturgical frivolity.

~

A corrective is called for, and appears. History is stopped in its tracks, then bizarrely reversed. The plagues that fell on others fall anew — this time on the distempered and disdaining — on ourselves. Life becomes a foggy flatland of enforced boredom: "In the morning one sighs, 'O for the nightfall'; and at evening, 'O when will morning come?'"

An anti-history; it is like a film, surrealistically played backward: "By sea, by ship, you will stream back" — to servitude, to the fleshpots, to the womb, safe and close, of tyranny.

~

The Exodus is told and retold, rooted in liturgy, in tribal memory.

Then something else, an opposite event. The freedom story vanishes in the thin air of a curse. Radically, ruthlessly, the original is rewritten. One history is erased; another is contrived.

Contrived — or real, this anti-Exodus, this humiliated return?

~

More, and worse. In Egypt those once freed remain, still slavish of mind — ". . . You offer yourselves in the slave market for a price."

And the final twist: "You will find no takers."

What to make of all this? Does the truth of events lie in the original text, or in the revision? That first word was all of freedom, of a god who intervened and liberated. We know it well, the glory of the Exodus.

Then, as though under a monstrous swing of the pendulum, the ancient story was revised.

"Revised"? The word is too neutral. The tale of Exodus was ground to a powder between upper and lower millstones. The grinders are variously named: deviance, injustice, reneging, violence, contempt for life.

~

And we have in hand an anti-story. It mocks, it smiles, a grimace of cruel irony. It tells of unfreedom, of a return to a demeaning (but oh-so-safe) place, a blind haven, a cave's maw, dark, ominous.

The people could not long abide freedom, or a god of freedom. They lusted after — bent backs, brick-making, slave masters, a tongue-tied litany of servitude. O for someone, some system to take us in charge, to indenture us, to provide a safe haven, to enforce a routine, an "order of the day"!

Also, of course, let us have full fleshpots, golden calves, the gods that promise security and a safe half-life.

Thus the original seekers after freedom retrogressed, sadly.

Egypt loomed once more, the unpromised land, the dark counter to the Promise That Was Too Much.

The cry: O set us free from this onerous freedom!

PART THREE

CALLING ISRAEL TO COVENANT FAITHFULNESS

Moses' Third Discourse (Chs. 29:2–30:20)

Chapter 29

29:2-9

This discourse of Moses was pronounced, we are told, shortly before his death.

Age has conferred its crown; wisdom has sharpened the mind's eye. The ancient seer observes the plight of his people, this unruly adolescent tribe. He mourns all they have failed to attain.

Have they not witnessed — and more, been gifted with — the great *gesta dei*, the deeds of the god? They have; and they comprehend nothing.

Placed before us is a conundrum: our human makeup, a baffling lack and lapse — name us blind, deaf, halt, mute. Or it is as though a finger of death lay upon us, stilling the heart. Prophet and people are stalemated. Together they must await a gift that they are powerless to create or merit — call it grace, steadfastness, enlightenment, a third eye serene and seeing.

Moses speaks of it beautifully, a lament, a confession:

> *To*
> *this day,*
>
> *Yahweh*
> *has not yet*
>
> *given*
> *you*

a heart
to understand,

eyes
to see,

ears
to
hear.

"To this day." Moses reads the clock right; he takes correct soundings of time and place. Passage of time (what hour of day or season of year), geography of the wilderness (how far they have come, how far they still have to go) — these are secondary to the main issue: spiritual stalemate, lack, incapacity. Despair, all said.

And what of the gift? It is hardly nameless; it is his own endowment: "wisdom."

This alone will bring "success in all your enterprises." Beyond semblance and appearance flows a hidden stream, the source, the grace — favoring, fostering, refreshing the human.

~

It is as though times outwardly prosperous were no more than a yawn, time gone to seed, a stalemate in a wilderness. Nothing, literally nothing relieves the inner darkness, the void.

Hearken, then, to the sound of waters. Drink deep of that stream. Its name is Helplessness. Halt here, wait. Taste the bitterness.

Waters not of Lethe, not of amnesia. Rather, of a "season of the soul." This is the urgent call of Moses, a man most interior — a call to patient vigiling, until the Gift be given. On behalf of all, he urges; he too waits.

~

His voice is his own, and not his own. There commences a mysterious wedding of tongues, a mystical mingling of two voices in one; that of the god and of Moses.

The apotheosis of the prophet nears. Nothing strange (but still, passing strange) — the god, about to take the holy one to himself, speaks through Moses — a hyphenated voice, a voice on-behalf.

~

Then the tone changes; resentments, like noxious weeds, spring. The voice grows querulous. If the people are thick-skinned, the god is all but skinless.

Are they forgetful, neglectful infants? They are.

And the god? He is a kind of memory bank: he forgets nothing, not an iota of benefit lavished on these indifferent ones, neglectful of gratitude.

~

There begins another interminable list of wonders wrought on their behalf. First, the celestial whip that fell to favor their cause, the plagues in Egypt and after.

Of other benefits we've heard before — the manna, the water struck from rock. Of the legend, after years of hard wear — sandals and clothing intact.

29:10-15

In the camp, all attend the audience of the god — even foreigners, quasi-slaves, those assigned dirty work: "the hewers of wood and drawers of water."

The term is of interest, and raises questions. Ironically, the chosen have created a class of slaves in the image of their own enslavement. They were the original "hewers of wood and drawers of water." Now they place on others a like burden and humiliation.

Has misfortune created the will to inflict misfortune?

~

Another question: Does the forced labor of the Solomonic empire influence these verses, the scribe of a later era making his imperial point?

The god is present, and speaks at length.

What of those lowly "hewers of wood and drawers of water"? Is the deity offended by their condition? To all appearances, he is not; no objection is raised. Cannily, subtly, a hint is offered: the victors are free to mistreat the conquered. The corvée, too, bears a divine sanction.

Even in the Canaanite years, astonishingly, class distinctions are set in place. Some among the vanquished are spared — to the advantage of the chosen. Spared, that is, for permanent humiliation.

In any case, all assemble, all hearken, all are bound. And against the defaulting, fulminations multiply.

29:16-29

What of the future, whether of the tribe or of "those come from afar"? The latter worship idols. They know no better. But the chosen, ah — theirs is an ominous, mysterious freedom. They are free to be unfaithful.

～

Within our composition of place, we are presented with a subtext. We enter the far future. Foreigners come on a scene of absolute disaster. Wonderment and dismay! The chosen are brought low, the Promise canceled, the earth devastated. All this and worse comes to pass. Exile follows, an undoubted reference to the Babylonian disaster.

～

Nothing of the story of decline and fall can be thought arbitrary. Throughout Deuteronomy, drawn-out and thrice underscored, is the close connection between crime and consequence.

All Solomonic pretension and puffing aside, read, ponder the biography of the tribe: death undergone, death inflicted, the gods of death paid vile tribute. Then, yang following yin. Retribution.

～

Ezekiel, driven half-mad, afflicted with vision upon vision of the offense and the end, is our witness. He sees all lost: the proud temple is a rubble; exile and death are the common lot.

Then, in a fetid wilderness, a moonscape — among the dead, a breath, something stirs. Something over and above death, an event beyond, prescient, against odds prevailing. A Presence breathes mysteriously on the dry bones. Gradually and so painfully, conquest is underway: life surpassing death.

A conferring, an unmerited gift; a consequence, a "then." The bones, by virtue of what is to come, "then" are addressed — a "you." Then "you" stand and walk in human guise, reborn — with implications of remorse, purification, return.

"Human one, can these bones come to life?" . . .

"Thus says the Lord God to these bones: 'See, I will bring spirit into you, that you may come to life. . . .'"

I prophesied as he told me, and the spirit came into them; they came alive, and stood upright. . . .

"Say
to them,

'O
my people,

I
will open
your graves

and you
will rise
from them,

and I
will bring
you

back
to
the
land

of
Israel.'"

Ezekiel 37:3, 10, 12

Chapter 30

30:1-7

A noble passage, an exalted promise — and what echoes it starts in Christian Scripture! "God will circumcise your hearts and the hearts of your descendants, in order that you may love God with all your heart and soul; and so may live."

Paul puts the matter brusquely; his words reward attention by Jew and Christian alike: "Appearance does not make a Jew. True circumcision is not a sign in the flesh. He is a real Jew who is one inwardly, and true circumcision is of the heart; its source is the spirit, not the letter" (Rom. 2:28-29).

Exactly, one thinks; and much to the point of both traditions.

～

To keep to the image, it is God who wields the blade. Thus Eliot:

The wounded surgeon plies the steel
That questions the distempered part. . . .

A stark image of grace, more precious than an entire theological treatise. The initiative is not ours; the knife is in other hands. And what must be cut away, if the heart (more than a fleshly organ) is to resume its beat, symbol of a vigorous, sustaining love?

～

The "in order that . . ." written of by Paul. Grace has its entelechy; it is not given "for nothing"; it is not to be thought static or neutral. To the contrary, the Gift is all energy and radical enablement. The blind see, the deaf attend. Marvelous: the dry bones walk abroad, and the giving is a creation, a "bringing to being of that which was not."

~

Now and again this book of Deuteronomy all but self-combusts. Turning away from dross and contradiction and meanness of spirit, the text grows incandescent. A word shimmers on the page, as though illuminated by a monk of Kells.

Here, such a word: we are enabled "to love God" with all completeness, with every faculty. It is as though love became the form of what we name soul, as soul is the form of body.

Love as the form of soul — to this point: a sublime freedom from gravity, through grace.

Lifelong we stutter, at a loss for words. Then, by the gift of God, our inarticulate, inchoative longings are lifted up and up, to a truly godlike love. Hands not our own lift us up. Our love is transformed, becomes comparable to the love whereby God loves God, to the love whereby we are loved.

Sublime consanguinity of love! And to bring to a close the packed revelation: in virtue of this love,

> . . . *thus*
> *you*
> *may*
> *live.*

To live by the love of God which is the gift of God. To come alive, to seek life, to be a life-giving presence before God and one another. . . .

In no other way, exalted or debased, are we "to live."

God knows, we know that high culture offers both: the exalted and the debased. Live by cultivating the arts. New York City is a hanging garden of delights: opera, symphony, dance, Broadway, Lincoln Center, Times Square, museums, exhibitions, celebrations. Name it, and it is yours, full and brimming over. . . .

Every sun casts shadows. High culture comes at a price. Therefore, live from deep pockets; make big money, invest, buy, rent, sell, squander, hoard in the city where money talks as loud and final as an auctioneer's gavel, as a mayor's drone. . . .

~

"To come alive, to seek life" — a different summons, to be sure. Lively — which is to say, questioning, objecting, resisting, naysaying, going counter — amid the welter and chaos of a culture of death. This is the grace offered, its form today.

Clear the mind of debris! Not by genius shall we attain life, nor through high culture or sound income or dominant gender or acceptable race or superior education or public plaudit or prestige of family or nimble pen or tongue. Perhaps least of all, by virtue of virtue.

By none of these, separately or in concert, shall we live. To the contrary: in reliance upon these, in seeking justification through these, in making much of these, in summoning and clinging to these, in accumulating and glorying in these, a chorus of self-approval — we die. Bowed under the enslaving yoke of the culture, we die.

And inevitably, and by no means "also" — we kill. We summon death, our genie, the "universal solvent" of the self-damned.

30:8-10

Moses our seer invites us to a far-distant era, the time of the "second conversion." Glory days are long vanished. Exile is the dire prospect.

Then, mitigation and return. Tears are shed, harsh lessons absorbed. And against all odds (the odds laid down by the principality named death), a chastened people emerge, spiritually reborn. They take up the task of return and rebuilding — a culture, a religion, a life together.

And the god shows himself unaccustomedly benign.

The shadow of a threat may lie on the horizon, a cloud no larger than a hand. But for the vastly larger part, the god radiates a mood of blessing: fruitful womb, fruit of the earth — it is all one, in fact and in metaphor. The people have been tried fiercely in the furnace of the nations. They emerge, made of beaten gold.

~

At moments like this, coming on texts like this, one gives thanks for Deuteronomy — and breathes a sigh of relief as well. How blessed we are; what sublime insight lies before our eyes! We hear a wonderfully soaring paean to the law. A law not written on tablets of stone, but inscribed on the heart.

The text soars like music, in celebration of the human. Beethovian, a veritable ode to joy.

And Yahweh himself orchestrates the music,

> *taking*
> *pleasure*
> *anew*
>
> *in*
> *your prospering,*
>
> *as he*
> *took pleasure*
>
> *in*
> *the prospering*
>
> *of*
> *your*
> *ancestors.*

30:11-14

Now we have a capital letter: the Law is personified, newly revealed as a Law of love, and more. It includes nothing of the esoteric, the secret, the jealously apart. One need not range the heavens or traverse the oceans to come upon it.

No, this Law is immanent, accessible; it rests upon humans like an open hand, blessing all.

Only look — the "Word" (Jerusalem Bible), the "Thing" (JPS translation) — we note the change of vocabulary — is near as a heartbeat, a breath in the nostril:

> *It*
> *lies*
>
> *upon*
> *your lips,*

in
your heart —

that
you

may
do
it!

Has the matter been put more clearly, simply, with such finesse?

~

Echoes of this theology of the Word resonate in the prologue of the Gospel of John:

In
the
beginning

was
the
Word. . . .

We know the rest; we have It by heart. Alpha is Omega, our heart's desire, one: "In your heart, upon your lips, that you may do it."

This is the fusion of heart and hand, of desire and outreach, the apogee of the human, beckoning and gift — and heartwarming giving of thanks. Then, abruptly, "Do it!" The succoring of victims, the "orphans and widows and strangers at the gate."

The Law, the Word, so understood, does not lie wholly, even primarily "without." Our tongues celebrate it. The Word flows in our veins, our heart's blood. It is an inner light, an ideal steadfastly held, a cherished icon of the human, radiant, unmistakable, life-giving.

Now we have Him/Her by heart,

That
you

may
do
it.

Do it. Which is to say, in an inhuman world, behave humanly.

30:15ff.

Yet another famed pericope — famed, and rightly so. We are deep in the tradition of the "two ways."

And we note with admiration that a like teaching is underscored in the Qumran scrolls, and in the *Didache* as well.

"Two ways." One is reminded also of the vocabulary of the Acts of the Apostles. Evidently in that century there was offered ample choice of spiritual "ways." But in the Acts, distinctions are ignored — no beclouding the irenic clarity. The community of Jesus refers to itself simply as "the Way," or "the new Way."

~

In our Deuteronomy passage, the two ways are named. The alternatives are set out in verse 15: "life and prosperity, death and doom."

~

Later, in verse 19, the solemnity deepens, the mood darkens. Once more, alternatives are revealed. Like blades laid against emery, they cast sparks:

I
call

heaven
and earth
to witness
against you;

I
have set

before
you

life
and death,

blessing
and
curse.

Was there ever a more munificent tribute paid our freedom? It is honored — even when we choose to walk appallingly wayward.

~

God, as implied strongly, does not stand neutral amid the mire and fury of life. Nor does this God hold in hand a scales nicely balanced, the pans weighed with equal portions of "life and death, blessing and curse."

Hardly. God has chosen in the act of creation itself. Has chosen for us, in our favor. For life, for blessing. "God found that it was good."

(And what shall we Christians say of the choices made by Christ? Costly, so costly — ourselves chosen for life and blessing — so that we might choose in accord.)

From the moment of creation, on to the symphonic utterances of John's Gospel, the Word bespeaks a love stronger than death:

This
is my command:

Love
one another

as
I

have loved
you.

No
greater love

than
this:

to
lay down

one's
life

for
one's
friends.

John 15:12-13

The scales are weighed — in our favor, irrevocably: life over death, blessing over curse. And by like choices, we attain the dignity of godliness. Choosing in favor of life. And so choosing in a world given over in ethos and act to death. A world embracing, thus, the curse.

~

Many years ago I was welcomed into the home of a poor family in Baltimore. In the living room, I saw this. On the wall, a small banner of burlap was hung. On it, an inscription was woven in contrasting colors: "9 X DOWN, 10 X UP" ("Nine times down, ten times up").

I have seen no better, more vivid or exact formula of a prevailing blessing.

~

The choices commended in our text find little resonance in the "high cultures" of the world. Whether one recalls Solomon's Jerusalem, Babylon, Egypt, ancient Rome — or contemporary New York or Washington — other choices darken the air: perversity of will, crooked diplomacy, war.

These coruscating principalities learn little or nothing from the debacle that befell the spoliating ancestors. Nothing learned. The bootless game, "by whatever means," continues: having and holding at whatever cost to others — sanctioning and bombing, interfering, plundering, terrorizing. As these notes are set down, another anniversary of the bootless misadventuring in Iraq and Afghanistan looms close, a ghost of Gehenna.

We mourn and take resolve.

It is as though a genetic, socialized, politicized, militarized "original sin" were transmitted through the ages. (As though?) Blind and repetitious, imperial decisions contemn the divine mandate: death over life. Invariably, as goes without saying, the death of others.

So this befalls those who choose (write it again) curse over blessing.

~

And what of the church, guardian and interpreter of the gospel — or so it is claimed? Below, the letter of a Jesuit theologian to the president of the United States Conference of Catholic Bishops:

12 October 2001

Dear Bishop Fiorenza,

Many, many people wonder why so many of our bishops and cardinals are not expressing the same concern for defenseless human life in Afghanistan, Pakistan, and Iraq as they did in defending the lives of four-day-old embryos. Why are you and your brothers not invoking the principle of sanctity of life? Why do you not invoke the language of the option for the poor? Why do we not see any reference of "Evangelium Vitae" or, better yet, the Gospel? . . .

I am enclosing but one story, "Residents of Afghan Scramble to Flee Explosions," from yesterday's AP Press. I hope it prompts you and your brothers to ask whether U.S. actions are "measured," "reasoned," and "just." I hope it moves you to expand your notions of innocent life and the common good to include those elsewhere in the world, especially those among the poorest. I hope that it leads you to invoke the persuasive argument of sanctity of life and that you, once again, champion defenseless human life.

Would that today we had a voice like Dorothy Day's, which could remind you, our bishops, to remember what happens when you not

166

only fail to criticize but actually support the U.S. administration as it wages a war that harms and kills many poor civilians.

Richard Keenan, S.J., Professor of Moral Theology

～

God knows the imperial choices, abominates them. Hence the solemnity and severity of language.

God knows with what ease even the chosen choose badly, in effect joining "the nations" in misadventure and idolatry.

30:17-18

So a warning is issued — not to the nations, but to the chosen. It dwells on woeful consequence: "If your heart twists about, if you refuse to hearken and are led astray to bow before idols and to serve them, I declare to you today: you will certainly perish. . . ."

～

What the choice of life over death, blessing over curse entails, we know something of. We Christians have our story — to ponder, to live by. It concerns God, and a Word spoken in our midst. That Word commended a certain "way," lived and died in close accord with his teaching. The Word dwelt in his heart and on his lips. He chose in its favor.

What that choice cost, and what it continues to exact of the faithful in our lifetime — of this we are appallingly aware.

Or we are not. After the fact, the example, the Word spoken, the Way lived and died for — still, Christians may choose the part of more or less guilty bystanders, donning the protective coloration of the culture, ethically assimilated, anonymous, consuming, taxpaying, lockstepping. "Good Germans"?

And the leaders of the church are hardly exempt from the above. Many among them become, as in these awful years of pre-emptive war, the misleaders.

And those who hearken to their teaching — alas for them, for ourselves, the misled.

⁓

The disappearance of American Christians into the culture goes largely unnoted and unreproved. As a body, we can choose to "fit in," enlisting for war when required, compliant, paying up, voting in favor of this or that political nonentity.

Let us suppose that the candidate — to the judiciary, the Congress, the White House — is a Christian. Most are — or so it is vehemently declared. He or she enters the dollars-for-media chase; win or lose, in the course of the campaign a huge "war chest" is amassed.

Whatever the political party, these masters of human fate ensure the prosperity of a few, the misery and death of many. Here is the unspoken, unprinted "platform" of whatever politician, seeking high office: Ensure the continuity of a system of inequity and cruelty, manipulate an ugly retributive public mood, tighten the coils of law and order. And undertake war, and not as a last resort — as a first, and only.

Let it be stated plain: The religion that goes with a culture of death goes down with the culture. We see it, or we do not: religion, culture, rotting before our eyes.

⁓

We will strike when and where required. We refuse all negotiation.
George Bush, 16 November 2001

⁓

Then, a sigh of relief. There exist far different Christians, the resisters of our lifetime, those who speak the Word, walk the Word, and pay up. Whose choices — life over death, blessing over curse — cut to the biblical bone.

Consequence follows as night the day. In the frosty eye of the system, these must endure judgment under the law of the land. They are criminalized and imprisoned. Including my Jesuit brother Stephen Kelly, my brother Philip, and many others. All honor to them, who hold the Word in honor!

⁓

Deuteronomy, we note, takes a long view, envisions a further outcome. The moral universe is patient, but not forever. The sublime Law is potent; retribution is inevitable. The crimes of the principalities turn and turn about, like a boomerang in mid-flight. Death, "the curse," comes howling home. The empires self-destruct.

The sublime threnody of Revelation 18 is the obituary of every empire — including, be it named, our own:

> *Fallen,*
> *fallen*
>
> *is*
> *Babylon*
>
> *the*
> *great. . . .*

Remarkably, in the text no enemy is adduced, no assault at the gates of empire. The implication is plain. Babylon, that exalted, luxurious high culture, fell like dough in a draft — of its own weight, its inner contradictions.

30:19-20

> *. . . that you*
> *and your descendants*
>
> *may*
> *live,*
> *loving God,*
> *hearkening*
> *to that voice,*
>
> *holding fast*
> *to God.*
>
> *For that*
> *will mean life*
> *for you,*

and length of days
in the land

which he swore
he would give
to your fathers,

Abraham,
Isaac,
and Jacob.

One pauses in admiration. Here, by anticipation, is the voice, lucid and life-giving, of Isaiah, Jeremiah, Daniel, the voice of their God and ours. A sublime charge, a truly biblical humanism, a vision, a behavior commended, an ethic worthy of humans.

The blessing rests upon those who cherish and sustain the tradition, the ecology, the Holy, one another. Presence, mutuality, compassion, love of the land — all are implied, and by implication commended.

And with what relief, one notes — no dire threats, no recriminations mar the text. It is as though an adolescent humanity (and its god, likewise?), after long impasse and conflict, were surpassed. God and humans come of age. Love prevails over guilt and punishment, as a ruling theme and motive.

We have found one another, and it is good. Connections are urged; without them, as has become clear, a tradition of the human is etiolated and profitless. It withers and dies, absorbed into one or another morbid "system."

God knows, our lifetime has suffered a surfeit of this!

PART FOUR

THE LAST DAYS OF MOSES

Song of Tragedy, Song of Triumph (Chs. 31–34)

Chapter 31

31:1-26

We have here a pastiche of various traditions. It is as though the last words and days of Moses reverberated in the memory of the tribe, in differing tones, accents, and emphases. The message falls upon many ears; one hears this, another that. An immensely rich message! Not surprisingly, many responses are evoked, many changes rung.

And all hear aright!

~

The word *Finis*, traced by our scribe, lies near. Diminuendo of the Great Scroll, of its protagonist, his sublime rhetoric and visionary counsel. Moses has variously attained "one hundred ten" or "one hundred twenty" years. Small matter, literally; it is the symbolic age of the holy ones. (Ironically, a like symbolic sum of years is assigned to Egyptian sages.)

All honor to our Moses — audacious, forthright of mind and speech, a magister of holy protocol, a mystic whose faith moved mountains, moved the Maker of mountains.

~

Still, one matter clouds the otherwise glorious ending. It lies there, to all appearances beyond contention. With age, Moses has failed to renounce the old, unreconciled god of the anathema. Thunderous Jovian brows darken the concluding pages.

Ahead, we are told, just beyond the Jordan, lurks the enemy, who must be destroyed. The god "marches with his people"!

~

It would seem a sound contention: We have at hand a revisionist history, the memories of those who prevailed. Their triumph is recorded, as has been suggested, in a scroll assembled far later than the events recounted. Memories have been absorbed in the guts of time; those who "broke and entered" the Land of Promise are transformed in their descendants. They have become the imperialists of the line of kings.

These lay claim to the story, and skillful ideologues they are. They shade the narrative, highlight the (dubious) glory, distort, omit where required — all in accord with the ideology, the vaulting ego, the crown and scepter.

No wonder, then, that a violent god is presented, urging his warriors to bloody deeds, faulting and despising the losers. "See, with a spot I damn them."

~

We have raised the question before: Who speaks for the silent ones (better, for those put to silence), for the slain and their defeated gods?

The victors bury them twice, stripping them to "bones, dry bones."

As for the chosen, they prosper and hold heads high among the nations. The equals of the nations, and under Solomon the Magnificent, in pride of place, the greatest among the nations.

From an eminence of glory, prospering, bearing unassailable credentials from on high, the scribes survey the past, exalting the god even as he has exalted them. A wondrous exchange.

To the victor belong the memories. In the era of our narrative, the enemy is long disposed of, safe and silent. No survivors. The scribes of Solomon have ensured it: one version only.

~

And yet, and yet; there exists a counter to the overweening theme of glory. A smoke of anger issues from the Oracular Tent. Now, we are told, the pronunciamentos of the deity turn away from themes of love and life. The mood grows somber, grief-stricken, even ignominious. Moses will shortly die. Then the people of the covenant, the apple of the deity's eye, aided and abetted through crises beyond number — these will fall away, bowing to other gods — even to the gods of the Land of Promise.

They have learned nothing. So. A yang to this ignoble yin. Defeat, humiliation, and exile are inevitable.

31:27-30

Moses can scarcely credit his eyes and ears. He cries aloud to the Levites, "For I know your spirit of revolt, your stiff necks. And if even today, while I am among you, you are rebels against the god, how much more so after my death?"

What rebellion festers within? To visionary Moses, past and present are strangely intermingled. In his mind's eye, the people once more are refugees, standing at the Jordan, facing the crucial "crossing over."

And a faultless script falls and fails, in tatters. Do murmuring and muttering break out once more? Is a new golden calf forged? Do fleshpots lure them from the austerities of freedom? Something, some primal fault has shown face.

In prospect, much is lost. But all is not lost. This consolation abides: If a present generation proves renegade, we shall give them over, placing our hope in the unborn.

Thus Moses: Against the grain of an unpromising present, let us proceed. Promulgate the tradition, the sublime Law. More: Mount a celebration and compose a splendid canticle. Thus we shall open a broad venue, a grandiose procession toward the future. Knowing that life and love, having undergone great travail, at length shall prevail.

Chapter 32

32:1-43

The Canticle of Moses
Heavens,
  bend ear to my voice,

173

creation,
    attend me!
    Upon all things green and grand
my words
      fall like a dew.

I summon
      (dare the Name!) —
our Rock,
      our Stead amid storm,
    all Just, all Good!
        Yet
    see,
tares in the sweet harvest —
        perverse, cross-grained
    this tribe —
"Only remember," I pled —
    "Remember the first days —
how the good land
    God
      parceled out,
        to each, to every
    a freehold abundant —
    But to you
      more, yet more —
a cornucopia,
the creation
    whole, undivided,
      the Promise entire!

In the land of the steppes
God took you to heart,
    the heart of Yahweh,
      incandescent
    with song of songs.
      God bore you up,
    hovered over —
a majestic eagle,

wings outspread,
the eaglets
sheltered and safe.
Yahweh led you, no other,
from wilderness to Promise —
like arrows in air
(and who to hinder?)
you sped triumphant —
the Promise, the Promise!
Honey from rock oozing,
cream of peerless wheat,
from buttery cows, sweet milk,
lambs redundant, bounding
from fattened ewes,
gross rams,
horned, sounding shofurs,
Bashan bulls,
like black-browed,
muttering warriors,
goats
in rut butting —
blood of the grape
'beady bubbles
winking at the brim' —

you,
feasting like Dives,
sated, grown frisky,
gorged, belly protuberant —"

Yahweh speaks, mourning:
"Look, they
turn, turn away from Me,
stooping,
bowing,
supplicating their
gross abominations —

stillborn, soulless, faceless
stocks and stones —
What then?
    This:
        I
    wash hands
of a perverse
        progeny of Baals.
    Cover my eyes!
They flounder, falling
    — like Lucifer's clones —
    from grace, from
my face.
    They squat
        in lewd sanctuaries —
    their coven of idols, mere
zeros, block-
        heads, nonsensical
    nonentities!
    So be it.
I turn turvy
    the origins, the logic!
        Perfidy!
Are these then
    accounted 'the chosen'?
Hereby unchosen,
    disenfranchised, disdained,
their bizarre
    animations, unrealities!
    Anger, kindled in hell —
        earth, time, kindled for fuel;
    'The chosen'?
I toss them aside, brands
    for the burning,
I launch them like arrows
    far from the gaze of love.
    To hell with them!

A curse! —
Teeth of lions on prowl
bared against babes,
 sting of scorpions
  upon sweet-fleshed maidens!
  A pestle,
 I grind them,
 their memory a dust
  flung errant to wind.

  Sound wisdom
  would reason aright:
'Weak as the newborn,
 yet we prevailed,
  countered all odds —
how came it, one Israeli
routed a thousand, two
 ten thousand?
  Did not
  our Rock of Ages
  gather us,
   gargantuan,
 momentous —
Apocalypse, engorging
 the Last, the Consummation!
The enemy, their gods —
 a vine plucked from Sodom,
 from Gomorrah's plantations!'

 Still, these —
  all said, all suffered,
 are they not —
  (cancel it, my decree —
the 'former,' the 'rejects,' the
'defaulters of debt'
canceled;
 the unchosen,
 the disenfranchised,

the disdained)
— my arms ache for them, eyes
drown me in tears —
    are they not,
    all said,
        crown
        of my sumptuous creation?
See how they fail,
those idols —
    mock-ups, papier-maché
godlings, fallen
    to tatterdemalion.
    Come now, you
    rocks, you gods.
    Come now, votaries —
        parade before me
        huffing and puffing,
            these puppets!
        I affirm, I smile, I surpass.
    Your idols
        strut upon the hour,
    out of time's entrails
issuing, vanishing —
    witless, sightless,
    going,
    going,
    gone —
into the maw of darkness.

Yahweh
    abides, affirms,
    ageless, availing,
a buddha surpassing
        you —
        appetitive,
        mewing infants,
    sucking
    thin milk at breast —

specious immortality.
Immortality?
I raise my hand
to high heaven,
— tremble, angels, archangels,
great seraphs, quail! —
I swear
by supernal Yahweh
(no other
in heaven's vault, on earth,
in hell's dark dominion —
no other invoked) —
Swear it, my soul.

Exult, ye heavens,
Ye nations, in chorus —
pay fealty, due honor
to Yahweh —
no other!"

32:44-47

"The law is your life," Moses concludes. A beautiful phrase sums up the theme of the discourse.

How then reconcile the Mosaic statement with that of Paul, to the effect that "one is justified by faith, apart from observance of the law"? (Rom. 3:28).

Perhaps this is the clue, a clue as ancient as the vision of Isaiah. Paul questions. A grand flourish of rhetoric sweeps all before: "Does God belong to the Jews alone? Is he not also God of the Gentiles?" And he answers, with the assurance of a seer: "Of the Gentiles too!" (3:29).

And again, summing up and, at the same time, denying (or dissolving) the conflict: "Are we then abolishing the law by means of faith? Not at all; to the contrary, we are confirming the law" (3:31).

~

Perhaps we can justly say that in his era, Paul is placing the law in perspective. The protagonist of his letter is a Gentile. A convert, he has yielded before a saving act occurring long after the time of Moses: the death and resurrection of Christ.

Jew or Gentile, circumcised or not, all are justified by faith in the same God (3:30). In a contrasting logic, no one is self-justified, whether through culture, gender, race, education, ego, religion — or the law.

Sic solvitur — at least according to Paul.

~

Let us translate that "justified" of Paul. It comes to something both simple and sublime: We are granted to know the truth of God and of one another. Knowing, submitting to the truth of a God who loves us, of brothers and sisters whom we are summoned to love.

And by the same Gift and in due time, we shall see God.

The Gift underscores our dignity and our helplessness as well. Without the Gift, we cannot give. We cannot love, cannot even be convinced that we are loveable.

Talk about hell on earth. Or a possible heaven?

~

In any case, for the faithful, conflict within and without. Therefore the cry:

> Batter my heart, three-personed God; for you
> As yet but knock, breathe, shine, and seek to mend;
> That I may rise, and stand, o'erthrow me, and bend
> Your force to break, blow, burn, and make me new.
> I, like a usurped town, to another due,
> Labor to admit you, but O, to no end!
> Reason, your viceroy in me, me should defend,
> But is captived, and proves weak or untrue.
> Yet dearly I love you, and would be loved fain,
> But I am betrothed unto your enemy.
> Divorce me, untie, or break that knot again;
> Take me to you, imprison me, for I,
> Except you enthrall me, never shall be free,
> Nor ever chaste, except you ravish me.
>
> John Donne

~

It bears repeating: Nothing can be thought to render us holy, acceptable to God or bearable to ourselves, apart from the Gift.

Too, by virtue of the Gift, we glimpse the Otherness of the Giver, who, in a clumsy phrase, is "culturally unassimilable," "not to be put in harness." This God is unentailed, disdains imperial pacts, economies, wars — and yes, religions. True God, transcendent — which is to say, useless to the trumpery plans and pacts of mortals.

None shall succeed in making of the utterly Other an entity known as "our god," a national god, the god of the military, of chaplaincies, flags in sanctuaries, Te Deums, "national cathedrals," and suchlike follies.

The close melding of self-interest and effort gone awry, were it to prevail, in effect would cancel the sovereignty of the Holy, cancel out the capital "Name above all names." Would declare the god, in effect, a national (and, inevitably, a military and economic) idol. The idol of our hearts' murky craving.

~

We have seen it, and are sick at heart: an anti-biblical ethic, the drive and misdirection of American culture. To own, control, and exploit the transcendent One.

Still, there is hope. A biblical people take up the glory and shame of resistance. Shortly, inevitably, they taste the bitter cup. "Let it pass from me?" It will not pass. They drink, and hand it to us.

~

Efforts to dominate God, to own, to manipulate, to hold the Divine hostage — these loose a torrent of cultural justifications. Each is a sedulous ape of the Gift.

Thus we Americans justify ourselves, heaping credit upon credit. We are purportedly generous, forgiving, slow to anger, quick to offer relief to the afflicted, and so on.

The official rhetoric declares the nation heir to the Promise, America as the Land of Promise. The national idol confers justification: citizenship in the land of the free.

But the purported benefit serves only to inflame: it engenders conflict, placing the citizen-believers in contention with the "non-chosen" elsewhere on the planet. Again and again, war follows, the international form of domestic idolatry. If the superstate is to remain "number one," "the indispensable nation," shows of force must constantly be contrived.

There exist, of course, other nation-states, with their competing ideologies and interests. And, as we have learned to our lasting sorrow, there exist throughout the world more or less hidden bands of malcontents, their resentment verging on the suicidal. In the autumn of 2001, as the world knows, they struck with deadly force, and many in our midst died.

~

In Deuteronomy, the national god of the Israelites gives the game away (perhaps unwittingly?). We have heard it before, an argument cleverly turned by Moses: If the warriors of "the chosen" do not prevail, their god will be held in scorn by the gods of contending nations. In heaven as on earth, this is intolerable.

32:48-52

Here and there, as the story unfolds, the humanity of the god shines from the page. We have seen it, and been consoled, this momentary break of sunlight in a fog-ridden day.

A word of compassion sits on the page, an orphan among wolverines. The deity knows a deep, mournful longing: that the love he bestows be requited.

Or we hear a wholehearted word of forgiveness, of good pleasure in the flourishing of the recusant — who remain, despite all, the chosen.

And that sublime assurance: the Word is "near at hand," available, amiably wrought, of human scope. How helpful, how empowering: the Word, seriously taken, urges virtuous behavior.

~

For a moment, the god is transformed. Now he is utterly Isaian: a hand stretches forth, compassionate and welcoming, from the Cloud. If the chosen would truly be accounted his own, in godly fashion they will mime his spirit. They will succor the stranger, the defenseless, the victimized.

~

The benign lineaments are, alas, never clear for long. Fog rolls in once more, and chills to the bone.

The god shrugs off his better part like a superfluous garment. Distemper, a mood of vengeance and violence surges back. He will have his sway — his prey, this wolverine.

In this mood the god never forgets, and seldom forgives. The anathema — and a sword is unsheathed.

We are puzzled and shocked at this double mind. We sense that the god has failed us, has failed to be — God. Failed as well to arouse and validate the better instincts of his tribe.

We long for the God of Jeremiah and Isaiah, the psalms that celebrate compassion and new beginnings, in heaven as amid ourselves.

~

To our story. The crossing of the Jordan is imminent. For the wanderers, a generation born in the desert, the moment is one of unalloyed triumph.

For Moses, a far different outcome, unutterably bitter.

It is the end. He has sinned; he must pay up. A final instruction of the god is issued. Moses is to ascend Mount Nebo; from that eminence let him " . . indeed view the land at a distance. . . . But you shall not enter that land . . ." (vv. 49, 52).

~

It is as though the Promise were airborne, floating wondrous on the horizon. Afar, a green savanna, far as the eye can encompass — or weep for.

The prophet is dying. The fair land is desirable, unattainable; the mere sight must suffice. We marvel and mourn. Moses has given and given, of life and love, has endured and submitted — and received so little in return.

Never was the seer greater or more tragic than in the manner of his dying. His final prayer is a kenosis of obedience; it surpasses the narrowbored decree of his exclusion.

Chapter 33

First, Moses blesses Yahweh. In a sublime invocation, the god is honored for loving

> *the great*
> *ancestors.*
>
> *The holy ones*
> *are*
> *in God's hand.*
>
> *They fell*
> *at God's feet,*
>
> *they*
> *followed*
>
> *where*
> *God*
> *led.*

Then, one after another, the tribes are blessed, and to each is assigned its inheritance of duties and gifts.

Chapter 34

Perhaps it is with relief, sorrowful and secret, that Moses draws a last breath? The forty-year burden, carried with such nobility, is lifted from his shoulders. He dies in a good spirit, his greatness beyond cavil, his integrity unstained by the vacillation and default of his people (unstained also, one thinks, by the truculent spleen of the god).

Moses indeed can cry out, as a great descendant cried out in our lifetime, "I have climbed the mountain; I have seen the Promise. Free, great God, free at last!"